How Things Work
Encyclopedia

DK PUBLISHING

LONDON, NEW YORK,
MELBOURNE, MUNICH, and DELHI

Senior Editors Carrie Love, Penny Smith
Senior Designer Rachael Grady
Design team Lauren Rosier, Pamela Shiels,
Karen Hood, Hedi Gutt, Mary Sandberg, Sadie Thomas,
Claire Patane, Laura Roberts-Jensen, and Poppy Joslin
Editorial team Lorrie Mack, Elinor Greenwood,
Alexander Cox, Fleur Star, Caroline Bingham,
Wendy Horobin, and Ben Morgan
Picture Researcher Myriam Megharbi
Proofreader Anneka Wahlhaus

Consultant Roger Bridgman

Publishing Manager Bridget Giles
Art Director Rachael Foster
Category Publisher Mary Ling
Production Editor Sean Daly
Production Controller Claire Pearson
Jacket Designer Natalie Godwin
Jacket Editor Mariza O'Keeffe
US Editor Margaret Parrish

First published in the United States in 2010 by
DK Publishing
345 Hudson Street
New York, New York 10014

Copyright © 2010 Dorling Kindersley Limited

16 10 9
010-175932—Dec/09

A catalog record for this book
is available from the Library of Congress.

ISBN 978-0-7566-5835-9
Color reproduction by MDP, UK
Printed and bound in China

Discover more at
www.dk.com

Contents

There is a question at the bottom of each page...

How Things Work
Encyclopedia

DK PUBLISHING

LONDON, NEW YORK,
MELBOURNE, MUNICH, and DELHI

Senior Editors Carrie Love, Penny Smith
Senior Designer Rachael Grady
Design team Lauren Rosier, Pamela Shiels,
Karen Hood, Hedi Gutt, Mary Sandberg, Sadie Thomas,
Claire Patane, Laura Roberts-Jensen, and Poppy Joslin
Editorial team Lorrie Mack, Elinor Greenwood,
Alexander Cox, Fleur Star, Caroline Bingham,
Wendy Horobin, and Ben Morgan
Picture Researcher Myriam Megharbi
Proofreader Anneka Wahlhaus

Consultant Roger Bridgman

Publishing Manager Bridget Giles
Art Director Rachael Foster
Category Publisher Mary Ling
Production Editor Sean Daly
Production Controller Claire Pearson
Jacket Designer Natalie Godwin
Jacket Editor Mariza O'Keeffe
US Editor Margaret Parrish

First published in the United States in 2010 by
DK Publishing
345 Hudson Street
New York, New York 10014

Copyright © 2010 Dorling Kindersley Limited

16 10 9
010-175932—Dec/09

A catalog record for this book
is available from the Library of Congress.

ISBN 978-0-7566-5835-9
Color reproduction by MDP, UK
Printed and bound in China

Discover more at
www.dk.com

Contents

Technology

Hard at work

Getting around

There is a question at the bottom of each page...

About this book

The pages of this book have special features that will show you how to get your hands on as much information as possible! Look for these:

The **Curiosity quiz** will get you searching through each section for the answers.

Become an expert tells you where to look for more information on a subject.

Every page is color-coded to show you which section it is in.

weird or what?

These buttons give extra weird and wonderful facts.

Inventions

Any new idea or product that has been created by a person can be called an invention. Inventions change the way people live their lives—they make things safer, easier, faster, or cheaper.

Accidental ideas

Inventions can happen by accident. Chemist John Wesley Hyatt was trying to find a material for billiard balls. He spilled a liquid that dried into a tough, flexible film—"celluloid" that was later used as camera film.

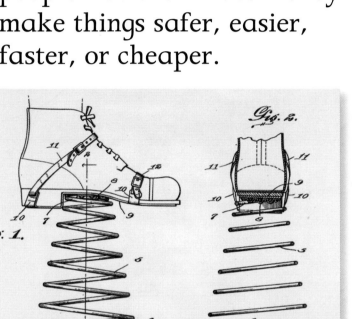

Knowing your stuff

Technology is the science of how things work. The inventors of these shoes knew that a coiled spring is a source of stored energy. They used this technology to make powered shoes.

Expensive origins

Some of the things in everyday use were developed for the space program. Smoke detectors, for example, were first used on *Skylab*.

"Discovery consists of seeing what everybody has seen and

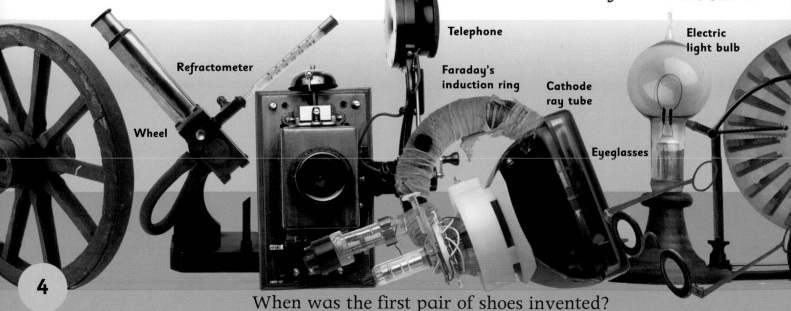

Wheel

Refractometer

Telephone

Faraday's induction ring

Cathode ray tube

Electric light bulb

Eyeglasses

When was the first pair of shoes invented?

I can find a use for that!

Some inventions end up very different from what was planned. Scientist Dr. Spence Silver invented a glue that wasn't sticky enough, so he thought it was useless. But his coworker Art Fry used it to stick bookmarks into his hymn book. The bookmarks wouldn't fall out, but they could be moved around. And so the sticky note was born!

Inventors

Inventors are creative people. The Italian artist and scientist Leonardo da Vinci was an avid inventor. He designed hundreds of machines, including airplanes, pumps, and cannons, that were centuries ahead of their time.

The first military helicopter, designed by Igor Sikorsky, took to the skies in the 1940s.

Leonardo da Vinci sketched a design for a helicopter 500 years before the first successful plane flight.

How long does an invention take?

An invention has to begin with an idea. It can sometimes take hundreds of years before the science, technology, or materials are advanced enough to make the idea work. The idea for a helicopter may have come from China as far back as 400 BCE.

Electric guitar

thinking what nobody else has thought." Albert Szent-Györgyi

Wimhurst voltage generator

Camera

Teamaker

Microscope

In 1500 BCE, people in Mesopotamia made the first leather shoe.

Better by design

Anyone can be an inventor. Many successful inventions came from engineers who used their knowledge of materials (such as iron) to try new things.

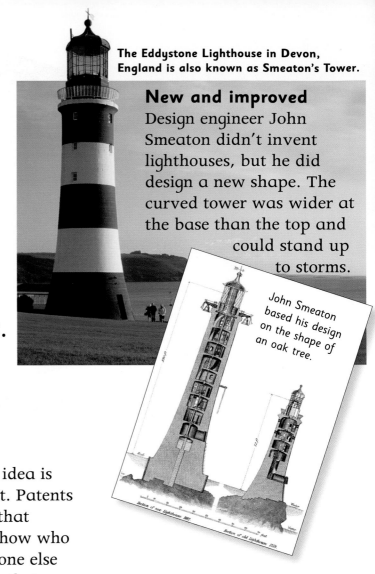

The Eddystone Lighthouse in Devon, England is also known as Smeaton's Tower.

New and improved

Design engineer John Smeaton didn't invent lighthouses, but he did design a new shape. The curved tower was wider at the base than the top and could stand up to storms.

John Smeaton based his design on the shape of an oak tree.

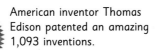
American inventor Thomas Edison patented an amazing 1,093 inventions.

That was my idea!

If someone thinks their idea is good, they can patent it. Patents are official documents that describe the idea and show who came up with it, so no one else can steal it and say it's theirs.

From that...

Since the telephone was invented more than 130 years ago, people have changed the design to make it better. Early telephones were large and boxy. Making a call may have involved winding a handle or turning a dial.

When was the first telephone patented?

Meet an engineer

Isambard Kingdom Brunel was a 19th century engineer who designed bridges, tunnels, ships, and even an entire railroad. He worked a lot with iron and knew it could be used in ways that had never been tried before.

Brunel's Royal Albert Railway Bridge was built in 1859. It's the only one of its kind.

Will it sell?

Even the best inventions can fail if people don't want what you've made.

 Sinclair C5 Failure. Not many people wanted to buy a battery-powered tricycle.

 Lego Success! These plastic bricks are one of the best-selling toys in the world.

 Microwave oven Success! It has completely changed the way many people cook.

 Sneakers Success! Can you imagine playing sports in any other shoes?

Making a difference

The way something looks can be just as important as how it works. The first colorful Apple iMac design made it stand out from other computers, so more people bought it.

... to this!

Today's cell phones are tiny by comparison, and you can do much more than just talk on them. You don't even need to use your hands to call a friend.

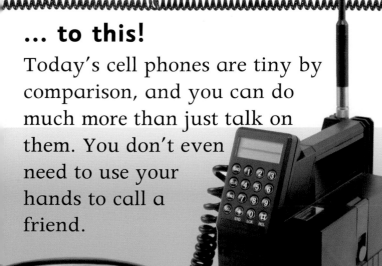

What will they think of next?

Alexander Graham Bell registered the patent in 1876.

Early inventions

Some discoveries and inventions seem so basic it's hard to imagine life without them. Yet someone had to be the first to create fire, wheels, shoes, paper...

c. 2000 BCE
Spoked wheels were lighter and more useful than solid ones. Two-wheeled chariots could move very fast.

c. 7000 BCE
For the first time, people knew how to start a **fire**. Later, they would be using fire in metalwork to create tools.

c. 3500 BCE
The first **wheel** was made from solid wood. Experts think it was invented in Mesopotamia (modern-day Iraq).

c. 2500 BCE
Early welding involved hammering heated metal parts together until they joined. Now all kinds of metal objects could be made.

7000 BCE

2250 BCE

c. 6000 BCE
Reed boats were made from bundles of papyrus reeds by the ancient Egyptians, who used them for trade.

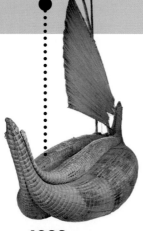

c. 3000 BCE
Reed pens and brushes were used by the ancient Egyptians for drawing signs on papyrus (which was used before the invention of paper).

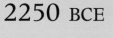

c. 2500 BCE
The first specially made **mirror** was made of polished bronze. Before then, people could see their reflections in water.

c. 1700 BCE
Evidence of early **plumbing** (drains and pipes) can be found among the ruins of the Palace of Knossos, on the island of Crete.

c. 4000 BCE
Wooden **plows** were pulled by animals to cut and turn soil for farming.

What does the "c." mean by the dates?

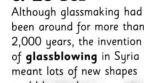

c. 1000 BCE
The earliest **underfloor heating** system is found in modern-day Alaska. The Romans invented their own system in Europe around 500 years later.

c. 500 BCE
The Greek **abacus** was a table with counters that people used to make calculations. Today's familiar abacus with rods and beads was invented in China almost 2,000 years later.

c. 300 BCE
The Chinese discovered that a free-moving magnet will point north—and so the **compass** was born.

c. 1000 BCE
The first **magnets** were simply lumps of magnetite, a naturally magnetic mineral. Modern magnets are made of steel.

c. 50 BCE
Paper was invented in China more than 2,000 years ago, but the invention was kept a secret for 700 years.

1200 BCE

100 BCE

c. 1500 BCE
Most early peoples wore sandals, but in Mesopotamia people crafted leather **shoes** to protect their feet.

c. 640 BCE
Before the first specially made **coins**, people paid for goods with beads, shells, tools, and even deer skins!

c. 200 BCE
The **Archimedes screw** is named after the Greek scientist Archimedes, who explained that water can travel upward along a turning screw.

c. 20 BCE
Although glassmaking had been around for more than 2,000 years, the invention of **glassblowing** in Syria meant lots of new shapes could be made.

c. 1200 BCE
The first **ships** were built by Phoenicians and Greeks to carry large amounts of cargo for trade.

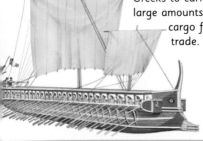

It stands for "circa," which means "approximately."

Modern technology

Today, the phrase "modern technology" is usually used to mean computers. But a few hundred years ago, steam power and mechanical presses were new and exciting technology.

1455
Before Gutenberg's movable type and **printing press**, books were copied by hand. Now they could be produced more quickly.

1565
Historians think the first **pencil** was invented by Conrad Gesner in Germany.

1608
In Holland, Hans Lipperhay invented the **telescope**—although some people think his children made one while playing!

1826
The first **photographic image** was taken by Joseph Niépce in France. He had to leave his camera still for 8 hours!

1400   1500   1600   1700   1800

Important ideas

Sometimes one invention leads to so many others, it changes the world.

1700s
The first machines and factories used to mass-produce goods led to the **Industrial Revolution.**

1800s
For the first time, people could safely harness the power of **electricity**.

1970s
The **microprocessor** made computers smaller and started the information age.

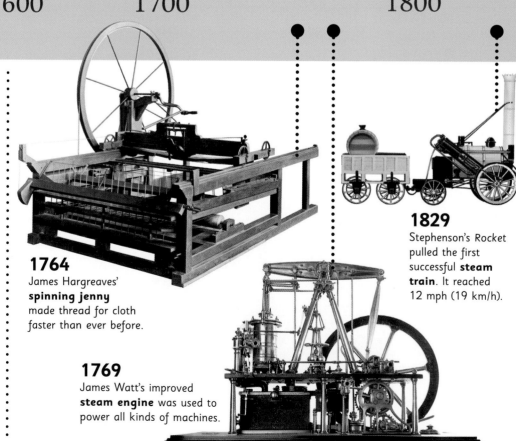

1764
James Hargreaves' **spinning jenny** made thread for cloth faster than ever before.

1769
James Watt's improved **steam engine** was used to power all kinds of machines.

1829
Stephenson's Rocket pulled the first successful **steam train**. It reached 12 mph (19 km/h).

Why was the printing press so important?

Modern technology

1903
The **first powered flight** took place in the US. The plane, the Wright Flyer, was made of wood and cloth.

1877
The first **personal computers** were large, chunky machines that had very little memory compared to today's models.

1878
The **light bulb** was invented around the same time in two different countries—by Thomas Edison in the US and Joseph Swan in Britain.

1957
The Soviet Union's *Sputnik 1* was the first man-made **space satellite.**

1876
Alexander Graham Bell got the first patent for a **telephone**, although others nearly beat him to it.

1926
The **Televisor** was the first kind of television. It was replaced by electronic television in 1936.

1982
The first **compact discs** were jointly produced by electronics companies Philips and Sony Corporation.

1900

2000

1885
Karl Benz made the first **gasoline-powered car** in Germany. By 1896, there were 130 Benz cars on the roads.

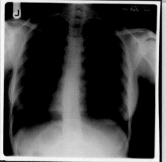

WWW

1990
The **World Wide Web** meant anyone could get information from across the world over the Internet.

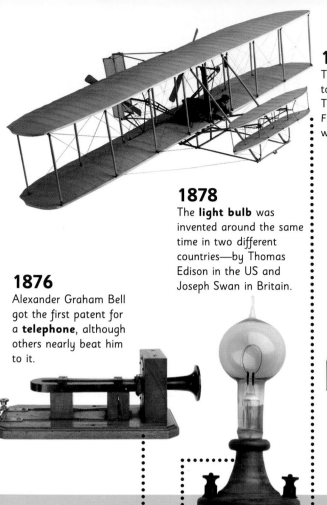

1895 German scientist Wilhelm Röntgen accidentally discovered **X-rays** as a way of seeing through tissue.

1938
Laszlo and Georg Biró's **ballpoint pen** had fast-drying ink and didn't need to be refilled very often.

1979
This year saw the first public **cellphone system**, in Japan.

1998
The first handheld **E-book reader** could store 10 books or 4,000 pages.

More books were made, so knowledge and ideas could spread more easily.

Technology all around us

The use of science to provide new and better machines and ways of doing things is called technology. Every day, you use technology in one of its many different forms. Here are a few of them.

Which technology is your favorite?

Become an expert...
on space travel, pages 54–55
on robots, pages 114–115

Mechanical

Mechanical technology is the design, production, and use of machines like wind-up clocks and other appliances that do not use electrical, electronic, or computer technology.

Chemical technology is used to make plastics and refine gasoline.

Chemical

When the science of chemistry is used to turn raw materials into more useful things like plastics, cosmetics, or drugs, this is called chemical technology.

Electrical

Technology that deals with electrical circuits and equipment is known as electrical technology. It is commonly used in the design and construction of machines and power grids.

How does nanotechnology get its name?

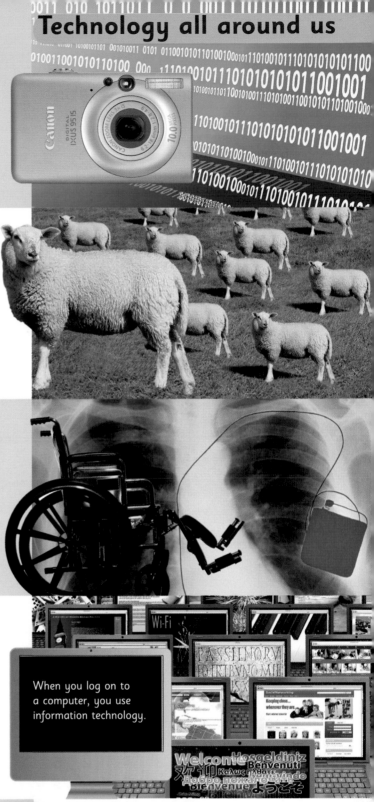

Digital

In digital technology, information is recorded using combinations of 0 and 1 to represent words and pictures. This system allows huge amounts of data to be squeezed into tiny spaces.

Biotechnology

This term refers to technology that is based on biology—the study of living things. Biotechnology is commonly used in agriculture and food production. Genetic engineering is biotechnology.

Medical

Anything (like a tool, machine, process, or substance) that is used to diagnose, observe, treat, cure, or prevent people's illnesses or injuries comes under the heading of medical technology.

Information

The study, design, and use of electronic information systems is known as information technology. The term covers machines like computers (hardware) and the programs they run (software).

When you log on to a computer, you use information technology.

Nanotechnology

Modern science can create materials and simple machines much too small for you to see under a normal microscope. This nanotechnology is used in products like special sunscreens and textiles.

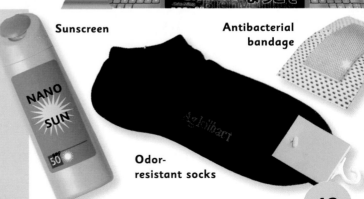

Sunscreen

Antibacterial bandage

Odor-resistant socks

13

"Nano" is Greek and originally meant "dwarf."

Simple machines

It's hard to hit a nail into wood with your hand, but much easier with a hammer. Tools such as this are called simple machines. They help people work faster and better.

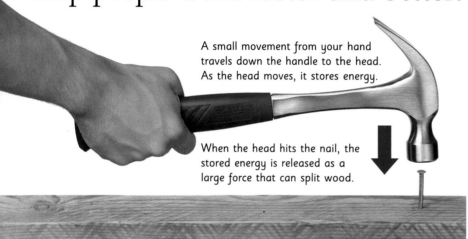

A small movement from your hand travels down the handle to the head. As the head moves, it stores energy.

When the head hits the nail, the stored energy is released as a large force that can split wood.

Feel the force

Tools, levers, and pulleys are all simple machines. They increase the size of the force you apply, so you can perform a job with less effort. When you use a hammer, you only need to move the handle a small way to give the head enough energy to push the nail through wood.

Levers move loads

Levers are simple machines that work by magnifying or reducing a force. A wheelbarrow is a kind of lever. It magnifies the lifting force from your arms so that you can lift and move much heavier loads. There are three different types of lever: class 1, class 2, and class 3.

Class 1 lever

Levers consist of a solid part that turns around a fixed point, called the fulcrum. In class 1 levers, the fulcrum is in the middle. The force you apply at one end is magnified at the other end.

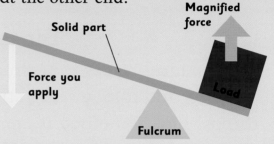

Class 2 lever

In class 2 levers, the fulcrum is at one end and your hands apply a force at the other end. This creates a magnified force in the middle.

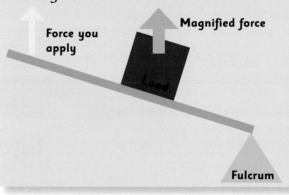

Class 3 lever

Class 3 levers reduce the force you apply. They are used in tweezers and other tools that pick up small, delicate objects.

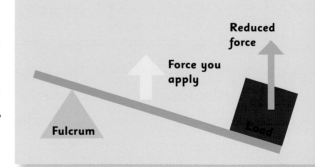

Fulcrum

A pair of scissors is made of two class 1 levers. You apply force with your fingers, and this force is magnified at the blades, giving them the power they need to cut through paper or other materials.

Fulcrum

A wheelbarrow is a class 2 lever. It magnifies the weak force from your arms to pick up the heavy load.

Fulcrum

The fulcrum in this pair of chopsticks is where they rest in the girl's hand. Her fingers apply the force that opens and closes the chopsticks to pick up food.

Pulley power

Pulleys are used to lift heavy loads. A pulley is a length of rope wrapped around a wheel. Adding more wheels to the pulley system creates more lifting force—but you have to pull the rope farther to lift the load.

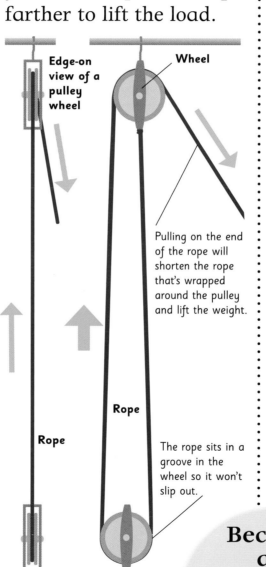

Edge-on view of a pulley wheel

Wheel

Pulling on the end of the rope will shorten the rope that's wrapped around the pulley and lift the weight.

Rope

Rope

The rope sits in a groove in the wheel so it won't slip out.

Rope

Curiosity quiz

Look through the "Hard at work" pages and see if you can identify the picture clues below.

Become an expert...
on cranes, pages 18–19
on conveyors, pages 20–21

The power that makes things move. Simply put—a push or a pull.

Using levers

Every time you open a door, ride a bike, or even bend your arm, you are using levers. Many of the objects we use every day depend on leverage to magnify forces and make tasks easier.

Magnifying forces

The amount by which a lever magnifies a force depends on how far the force you apply and the force the lever produces are from the fulcrum.

Levers at home

These are all compound levers—tools made up of more than one lever.

Nutcrackers are a pair of class 2 levers that are joined at the fulcrum.

Tweezers are made up of two class 3 levers. They reduce the force you apply.

Scissors are class 1 levers. The strongest cutting force is nearest the hinge.

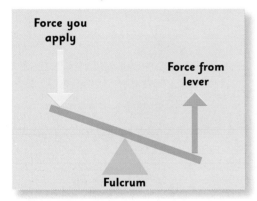

If the force you apply is the same distance from the fulcrum as the force the lever produces, the two forces are equal.

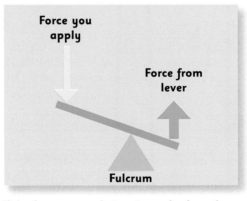

If the force you apply is twice as far from the fulcrum as the force the lever produces, the lever doubles the force.

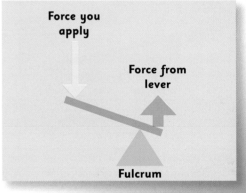

If the force you apply is three times as far from the fulcrum as the force the lever produces, the lever triples the force.

Crowbar

One of the simplest kinds of lever is the crowbar, which is a class 1 lever. You use a crowbar to prize very heavy objects off the ground. The longer the crowbar is, the more the force is magnified at the other end. However, you have to move the long end of the crowbar much farther than the short end will move.

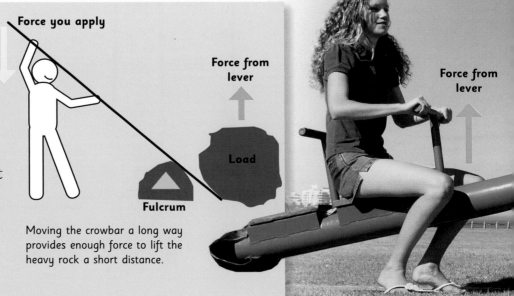

Moving the crowbar a long way provides enough force to lift the heavy rock a short distance.

Can you name other compound levers found around the home?

Human body

Your arms and legs are levers. When you stand on tiptoes, your lower leg works as a class 2 lever. The powerful calf muscle pulls up your heel, lifting your body weight (the load), while your toes form the fulcrum.

Force you apply

Load

Fulcrum

Fishing rod

When you use a fishing rod to cast a line, the rod works as a class 3 lever. Your hand applies a powerful force near the base of the rod to create a smaller force at the tip of the rod. Although the force is weaker, the tip moves much farther and faster than your hands, magnifying the speed.

Force you apply

Fulcrum

Load

The rod also works as a class 3 lever when you haul in a fish.

Seesaw

A seesaw is a class 1 lever. You use the force of your body weight to move the seesaw. If two people of equal weight sit at equal distance from the fulcrum, their weight will balance. But if one of them sits farther from the fulcrum, their weight is magnified and the seesaw tips over.

A small child could balance the weight of an elephant by sitting far enough from the fulcrum.

Force you apply

Fulcrum

Pliers are class 1 compound levers. Tongs are class 3 compound levers.

Construction work

Digging dirt, lifting loads—there's lots of heavy work to do on a construction site, and lots of large machinery to do it. Yet most of these machines use fairly simple science to do their jobs.

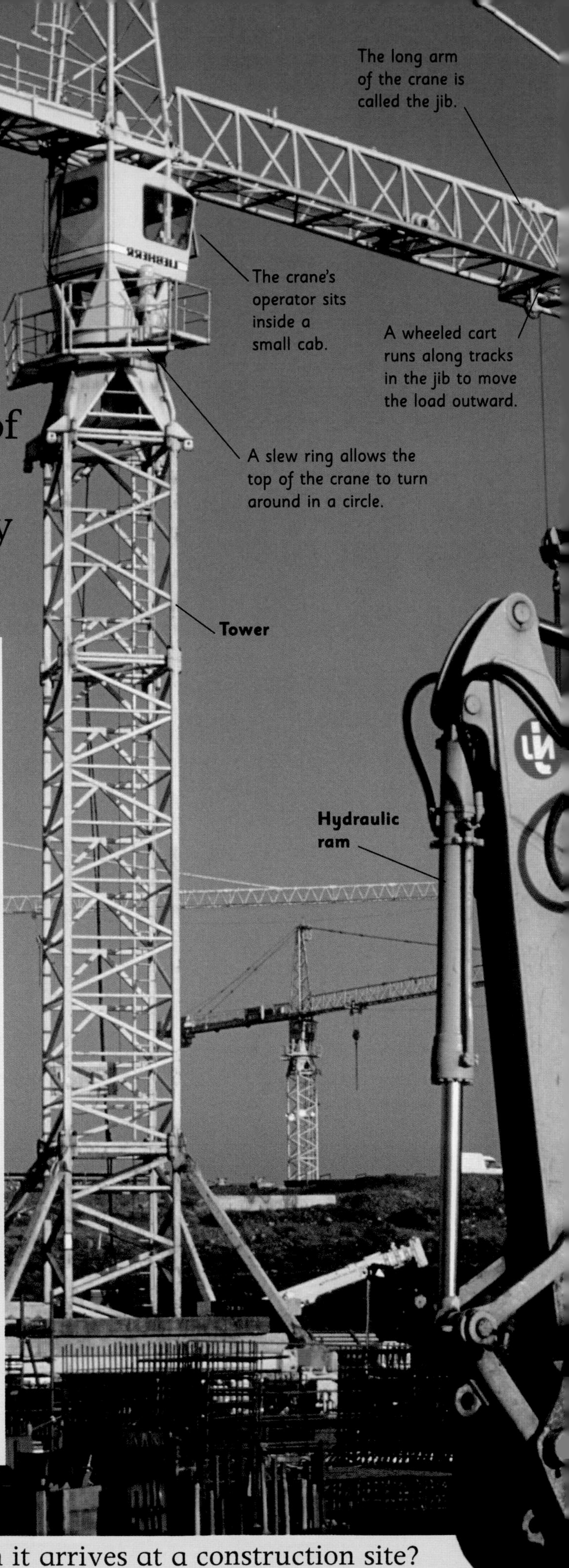

The long arm of the crane is called the jib.

The crane's operator sits inside a small cab.

A wheeled cart runs along tracks in the jib to move the load outward.

A slew ring allows the top of the crane to turn around in a circle.

Tower

Hydraulic ram

Why don't cranes fall over?

Tower cranes pick up and move the massive blocks of concrete and steel used to construct big buildings. A huge concrete "counterweight" on the rear arm of the crane balances the load carried by the main arm (jib). This stops the crane from toppling over.

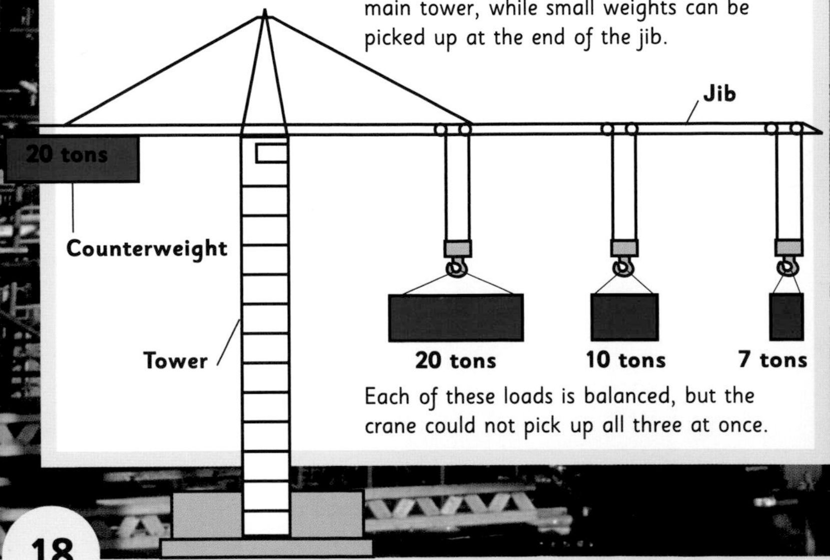

Large weights must be lifted close to the main tower, while small weights can be picked up at the end of the jib.

Jib

20 tons

Counterweight

Tower

20 tons | 10 tons | 7 tons

Each of these loads is balanced, but the crane could not pick up all three at once.

What is a crane's first job when it arrives at a construction site?

Pulleys in action

Cranes lift objects with a hook and pulley. A steel cable is looped around pulley wheels on the hook and jib and is wound in by a motor in the crane's rear arm. Each loop of cable magnifies the crane's lifting force.

Diggers

Diggers use a set of connected levers to scoop earth out of the ground. The levers are joined like the parts of a human arm, the bucket forming the "hand." They are moved by hydraulic rams—metal tubes that extend as oil is pumped into them.

Hydraulic ram

Hydraulic cranes

Mobile cranes, such as those on fire engines, are hydraulic cranes. Like diggers, they use hydraulic rams to transmit the force needed to lift loads. By varying the size of the metal tubes in the rams, the hydraulic system creates huge lifting forces—enough to raise bridges, trains, and even entire buildings.

Like pulleys and levers, hydraulic rams can magnify forces.

When the bucket is pushed inward, its sharp teeth dig into the ground to scoop out earth.

Boom

Slew ring

Bucket

The slew ring at the base of the arm allows the arm to rotate (turn around).

It builds itself, adding one section at a time to its tower.

Moving stuff

From airports and factories to stores and offices, conveyors are used in all kinds of places to make it easier to move loads from one point to another.

A gravity conveyor seen from above.

Move along

The simplest type of conveyor is a gravity conveyor. This is made up of lots of rollers or wheels in a frame. As each roller or wheel turns, the load gets shifted along to the next.

Luggage and other cargo are moved on conveyors behind the scenes at an airport.

Up, down, and sideways

Belt conveyors can move loads up, down, and sideways. The load sits on a belt that turns around rollers called pulleys. The drive pulley is connected to a motor, which makes it rotate.

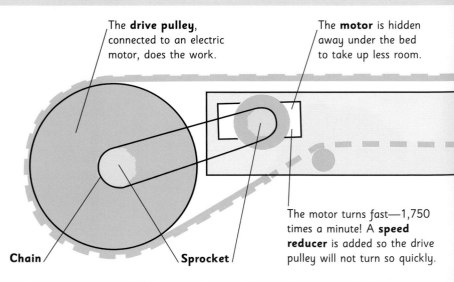

The **drive pulley**, connected to an electric motor, does the work.

The **motor** is hidden away under the bed to take up less room.

The motor turns fast—1,750 times a minute! A **speed reducer** is added so the drive pulley will not turn so quickly.

Chain

Sprocket

20

When was the first escalator used?

How to drive
The parts that make a conveyor belt turn are called the conveyor drive. Sprockets and chains are part of this. The chain sits in the gaps between the sprocket's teeth so it doesn't slip. When the motor sprocket turns, the chain moves and turns the drive pulley sprocket.

Sprocket

Going up!
It's not just boxes that are moved around on conveyors—people are, too. Escalators are moving staircases with each separate step connected to a conveyor belt. Even when the steps turn around the belt, they always stay level.

An escalator can carry more than 10,000 people in an hour.

The **steps** are connected to two belts. Wheels near the top of each step follow the drive belt, which is turned by the motor.

The **handrail** is also turned by the motor so you can hold on safely.

The steps flatten out at the top and bottom of the escalator so you don't trip getting on and off.

Electric motor

Drive pulley

Sprocket

Inner rail

Drive belt

The **belt** loops all the way around the bed and pulleys.

Bed

To stop the belt from sagging underneath, it might be tucked around small rollers called **return idlers**.

The **tail pulley** turns by itself.

Guide wheels at the bottom of each step roll along the inner rail to keep the steps stable.

Tail pulley

21

The first working model was made in the US in 1895—as a fairground ride!

Getting around = Energy ▶

We can all use our legs for getting around, but they're a bit slow and won't take us far without making us tired. What we need is something that can get us from A to B fast—a vehicle of some kind.

But what does it take to get a car racing along a road?

Energy sources

To move or do any kind of work you need energy. We get energy from our food; vehicles use fuel or electricity.

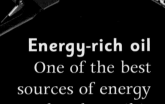

Energy-rich oil
One of the best sources of energy is oil. When oil is burned it releases lots of energy.

Types of fuel

Vehicles can get their energy from many different types of fuel:

 Gasoline is made from oil. Most cars run on gas burned in the engine.

 Diesel is also made from oil. It produces more energy than gasoline.

 Electricity can be used to power some cars but is mainly used by trains.

 Solar energy comes from the Sun. It can be stored for use by cars.

What moves faster than anything else in the universe?

Force ➤ Movement

Getting going

Once you have enough energy, you can use it to create forces that will help you move. Forces are simply pushes or pulls.

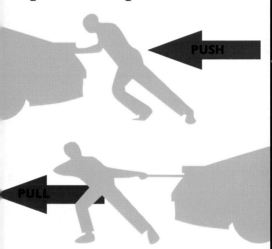

PUSH

PULL

Wheels turn by using opposing forces. As the tire pushes back against the road, the road pushes the wheel forward.

Friction

Friction is a force that stops things from moving by pulling them in the other direction. Without its gripping action, you couldn't walk or drive anywhere.

On the move

When you apply a force, things move. When you don't, they stay still. The greater the force, the faster something goes.

Speeding up

Speed is the key to getting somewhere fast. To increase your speed you need to be able to provide a lot of power quickly. A good engine and the right kind of fuel help.

Brakes work by pushing pads or disks against the wheels.

Slowing down

If you push against a moving object it will slow down and eventually stop. This is called braking.

Curiosity quiz

Look through the "Getting around" pages and see if you can identify the picture clues below.

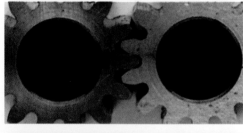

Become an expert...

on how bicycles work, 26–27

on car engines, 32–33

Wheels and axles

An axle is a simple rod that connects two wheels. For nearly 6,000 years, the wheel and axle have made it easy to move objects.

Friction

Friction is the force created when two surfaces touch. As you slide an object along, you create a lot of friction. When you roll it on wheels, you create less.

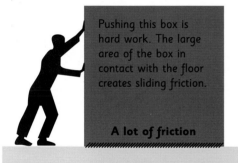

Pushing this box is hard work. The large area of the box in contact with the floor creates sliding friction.

A lot of friction

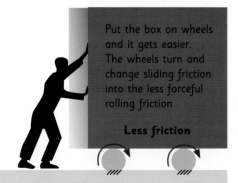

Put the box on wheels and it gets easier. The wheels turn and change sliding friction into the less forceful rolling friction

Less friction

Fixed axle

A fixed axle can be found on simple carts. The axle is attached to the cart and the wheels turn independently, allowing the cart to move.

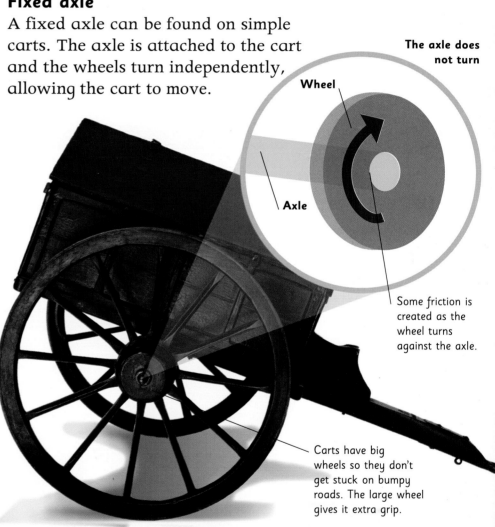

The axle does not turn

Wheel

Axle

Some friction is created as the wheel turns against the axle.

Carts have big wheels so they don't get stuck on bumpy roads. The large wheel gives it extra grip.

History wheels

Historians believe the very first wheels were used 8,000 years ago by potters to make pots. Then the wheel was used to help move and transport objects.

The first use of wheels and an axle was on horse-drawn chariots around 3500 BCE.

Bicycles, which allow us to create our own power, have been popular for over 100 years.

What is the largest wheel in the world?

Spoke support

The little rods that connect the outer rim to the inner hub of the wheel are called spokes. They make the wheel lighter but are strong enough to take the weight. They also spread the weight evenly, and transfer power from the axle.

Outer rim

Spoke

Hub

Other wheels

Wheels don't just move you or your belongings. They have a diverse range of uses:

A steering wheel is the fifth wheel on a car and helps guide it.

Gears use interlocking "teeth" to transfer movement and power.

Pulleys and levers use wheels to pick up and move heavy objects.

Waterwheels create mechanical energy when a river's current turns them.

Rolling axle

Modern cars and vehicles use a rolling axle system. The axle is connected to the engine and helps turn the wheels.

The wheels turn with the axle

Wheel

Axle

Gears

Driveshaft

The engine turns a rod known as the driveshaft. This uses gears to transfer the engine's power into the axle.

The turning force created by the axle moves the wheel.

weird or what?

The tweel is a brand new car wheel that doesn't need a tire. Instead, it uses flexible spokes, which bend with the bumps in the road. The tweel will never get a flat like a tire.

In "two-wheel drive" cars, one axle powers just two wheels. "Four-wheel drive" cars are powered by both axles.

With the invention of the engine, bigger vehicles needed bigger wheels to help move heavy cargo.

After a few early designs, the automobile was built and its wheels were covered with air-filled rubber tires.

The modern-day wheel is a hi-tech device. Race cars use special wheels for different racing conditions.

The history of bikes

The dandy horse (1817) The first bikes had no pedals at all. Riders had to push them along with their feet until they came to a downhill slope.

The velocipede (1863) The pedals on this bike were fixed to its wheels, and it had no gears. This meant the wheel turned once for every turn of the pedal. It took a huge effort to travel fast.

The penny farthing (1872) These bikes got around the problem of fixed pedals by having a huge front wheel. They were faster but also dangerous—it was a long fall down from the seat.

The safety bicycle (around 1884) This was the original name for a bicycle with gears—the same basic design that is used today.

Pedal power

A bicycle is a lean, mean travel machine. Bikes are so efficient, they can turn 90 percent of the energy you put into pedaling into forward motion.

Get in gear

Bikes can have up to 30 gears. They are cogs, or wheels with teeth, that are linked by a chain. Using different gears makes pedaling easier or faster.

When a small gear at the front wheel is connected to a large gear at the back, the bike is in low gear. This turns the wheel slowly but forcefully, so is ideal for traveling uphill.

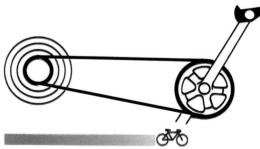

When a large gear at the front wheel is connected to a small gear at the back, the bike is in high gear. The wheel will turn several times for each rotation of the pedals. This is ideal for speeding along a flat surface or racing downhill.

The main picture shows a BMX bike. What does BMX stand for?

Bike types

Handlebars These are used to control the front wheel. Moving the handlebars lets you change direction and also helps you keep your balance as you cycle along. Handlebars are levers, and the longer they are, the easier they are to turn.

Brakes When you squeeze the brake lever on the handlebars, it pulls a cable that's connected to brake shoes on either side of the wheel. The rubber shoes grip onto the wheel like a clamp. This creates friction against the wheel, slowing it down.

Frame Most modern bikes have a "diamond" frame—a shape made up of two triangles of hollow steel, which is light but strong.

Pedals These turn the up-and-down motion of your legs into the circular movement of the wheels.

Tires Patterns called treads on the tires increase friction between the bike wheel and the road surface, so that the bike is easy to control and keeps a good grip, even in rainy conditions.

Wheels The spokes near the top of each wheel carry the weight of the bike and rider.

weird or what?
The world's longest true bicycle (one with just two wheels) was built in The Netherlands in 2002. It was 92¼ ft (28.1 m) long!

Utility bikes are used for everyday cycling. A chain guard stops the oily chain from getting your clothes dirty, and bags can sit safely in the front basket.

Mountain bikes have a strong frame and wide tires for extra grip on rough ground.

Track-racing bikes are designed for speed. The rider must bend low to hold the handlebars, making a streamlined shape. These bikes have no brakes!

Recumbent bikes have frames that make the rider lean back in their seat. Some have covers, too. They can be tricky to ride, but can go very fast.

27

Bicycle Motocross, a sport based on motocycle racing ("motocross").

Holding the road

Why do trucks and tractors need such big wheels? It's to help them get a grip on slippery surfaces and move easily while pulling loads.

Sticking to the surface

Heavy vehicles need big tires to help spread the weight of the truck and its load. It is the tires that move the vehicle, using friction. As the tires press down and backward on the road, the road pushes the vehicle forward.

Losing your grip

This car's wheels can't get enough grip to move. Mud is wet and slimy and does not have any snags and bumps to provide friction. The car's wheels are too small and smooth to provide enough surface area to reduce the pressure of the heavy weight of the car on the ground.

Tractors overcome this problem by having wide tires with deep treads that provide a better grip.

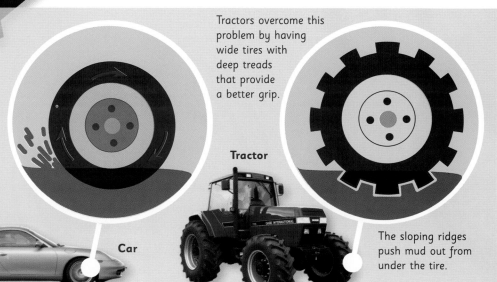

Car

Tractor

The sloping ridges push mud out from under the tire.

How big is the world's largest tire?

Monster trucks

What do you get if you put the body of a pickup truck on a bus axle? The answer is a monster truck. Add some tractor wheels and a good suspension system and you can bounce over anything.

Smoothing out the bumps

When you hit a bump in the road your wheels move up and down. The suspension system is designed to absorb the impact through the tires, springs, and shock absorbers.

Inside the shock absorber is a piston that pushes against a gas. The gas slows the piston down and turns its energy into heat.

Spring

Cross-section

Shock absorber

Tire

Tires

Tires are left slightly soft so they can squash over small bumps without moving up and down.

Springs

There is a spring around each shock absorber that reduces the impact by squeezing and stretching.

Shock absorbers

These are pumps filled with gas that absorb the energy of the wheel hitting the ground.

29

It measures 13 ft (4 m) across and weighs 8 tons (7.3 metric tons).

Piston power

Many forms of transportation use wheels, which push against the ground and use friction to move. But what makes the wheels turn?

Up and down, around and around

To ride a bike, you move your legs up and down on the pedals. The pedals turn cranks around and around to turn the wheels. A car's wheels move in a similar way.

Gear

Crank

Pedal

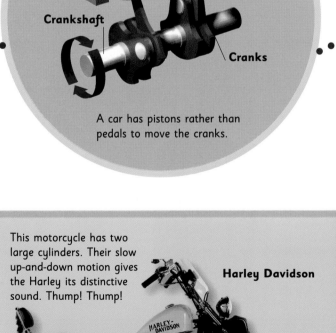

Cylinder

Pistons

Crankshaft

Cranks

A car has pistons rather than pedals to move the cranks.

Rear-wheel drive

A bike's cranks turn a chain that is connected to the back wheel, so when you pedal, you are actually only powering one wheel. Many bikes have gears to make pedaling easier.

Types of engine

Different vehicles have different numbers of cylinders. Generally, the larger the vehicle, the more they have.

A lawnmower has only one cylinder (so only one piston going up and down to turn the wheels).

Lawnmower

This motorcycle has two large cylinders. Their slow up-and-down motion gives the Harley its distinctive sound. Thump! Thump!

Harley Davidson

What is a "four-wheel drive" car?

Secret cylinders

There is a row of metal pistons hidden deep in a car's engine. The pistons pump up and down, just like your feet on a bike.

Start at 1 to see how the pistons power the wheels.

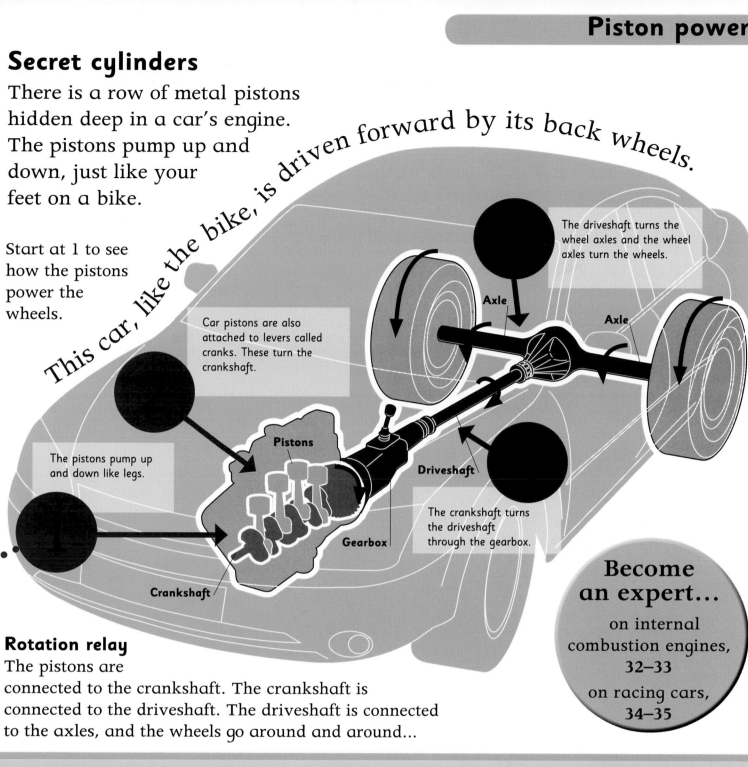

This car, like the bike, is driven forward by its back wheels.

The driveshaft turns the wheel axles and the wheel axles turn the wheels.

Axle

Axle

Car pistons are also attached to levers called cranks. These turn the crankshaft.

The pistons pump up and down like legs.

Pistons

Driveshaft

Gearbox

The crankshaft turns the driveshaft through the gearbox.

Crankshaft

Become an expert...
on internal combustion engines, 32–33
on racing cars, 34–35

Rotation relay

The pistons are connected to the crankshaft. The crankshaft is connected to the driveshaft. The driveshaft is connected to the axles, and the wheels go around and around...

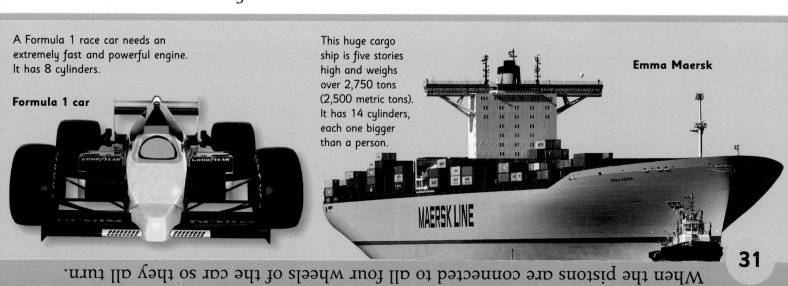

A Formula 1 race car needs an extremely fast and powerful engine. It has 8 cylinders.

Formula 1 car

This huge cargo ship is five stories high and weighs over 2,750 tons (2,500 metric tons). It has 14 cylinders, each one bigger than a person.

Emma Maersk

MAERSK LINE

When the pistons are connected to all four wheels of the car so they all turn.

Engines of fire

Cars, and other vehicles, must burn fuel to release the energy needed to move. This happens inside an "internal combustion engine"—an engine that is powered by lots of little fires.

What makes it burn?

Fuels such as gasoline and diesel burn easily. All they need are a spark and oxygen. Oxygen is found in the air.

Exploding with power

At normal speed, a car's engine lights around 50 little fires every second. The fires make pistons shoot up and down, with four "strokes" for every fire—suck, squeeze, bang, and blow.

Recipe for fire:

Fuel + oxygen + a spark = fire.

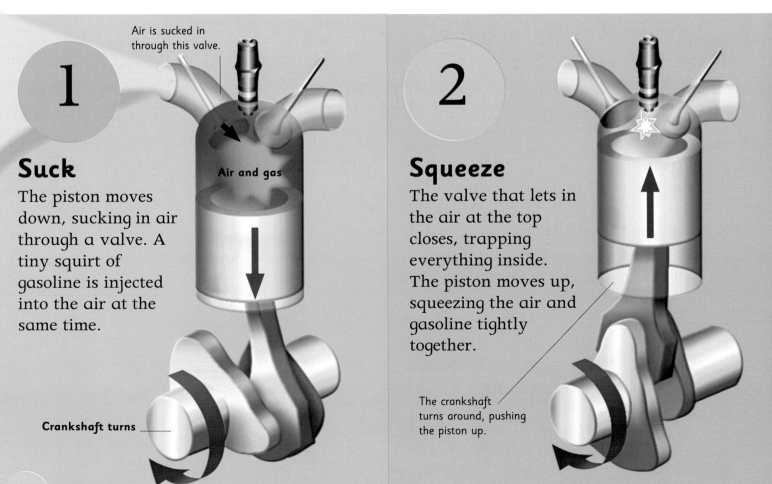

Air is sucked in through this valve.

1

Suck

The piston moves down, sucking in air through a valve. A tiny squirt of gasoline is injected into the air at the same time.

Air and gas

Crankshaft turns

2

Squeeze

The valve that lets in the air at the top closes, trapping everything inside. The piston moves up, squeezing the air and gasoline tightly together.

The crankshaft turns around, pushing the piston up.

What actually is fire?

The cylinders

The combustion (burning) happens in an engine's cylinders. The energy let off by each tiny explosion is directed to the pistons and causes them to move up and down. This drives the crankshaft around and around, turning the wheels (see pages 30-31).

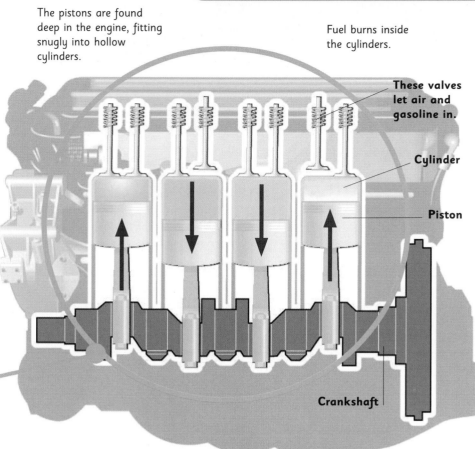

The pistons are found deep in the engine, fitting snugly into hollow cylinders.

Fuel burns inside the cylinders.

These valves let air and gasoline in.

Cylinder

Piston

Crankshaft

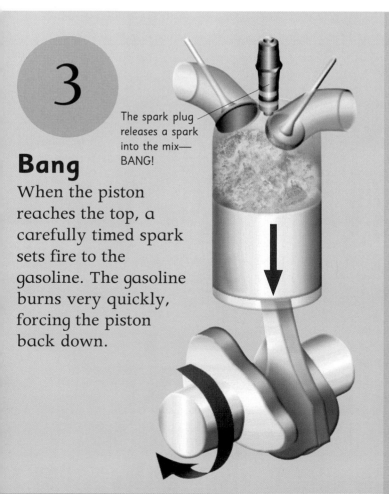

3

Bang

When the piston reaches the top, a carefully timed spark sets fire to the gasoline. The gasoline burns very quickly, forcing the piston back down.

The spark plug releases a spark into the mix—BANG!

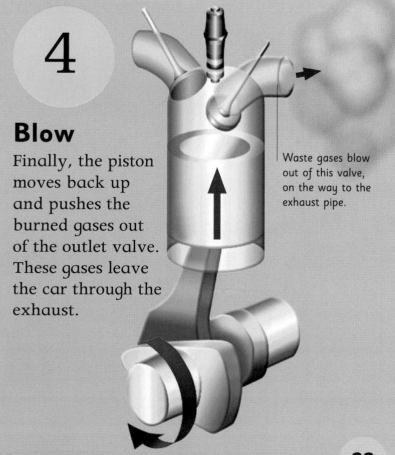

4

Blow

Finally, the piston moves back up and pushes the burned gases out of the outlet valve. These gases leave the car through the exhaust.

Waste gases blow out of this valve, on the way to the exhaust pipe.

It's a high-speed chemical reaction that produces heat and light.

Race cars

Formula 1 cars are like normal cars in many ways. They have gas engines, gears, and steering wheels. However, they are built with only one thing in mind, and that's WINNING RACES!

A technical masterpiece

Every bit of a Formula 1 (F1) car is light and very strong. At its peak speed of 225 mph (360 kph) air flows over it with the force of a tornado, so it is as low and streamlined as possible.

Pit-stop pressure
At pit stops, a driver refuels and gets new tires. This is all done in about 30 seconds. That's about the same amount of time as it takes to read this paragraph!

The car's spoilers create a downward force that stops the car from taking off at high speed.

Even the driver's helmet is part of the streamlining.

The blue arrows show how air flows over the car as it races.

What is the minimum weight of a Formula 1 race car?

G-force

A Formula 1 driver is shoved around violently inside his car as it twists around the track. A pushing force called g-force, which can be up to six times more powerful than gravity, shoves him backward, forward, and sideways as he races. You see g-force at work in a normal car by watching water sloshing in a cup.

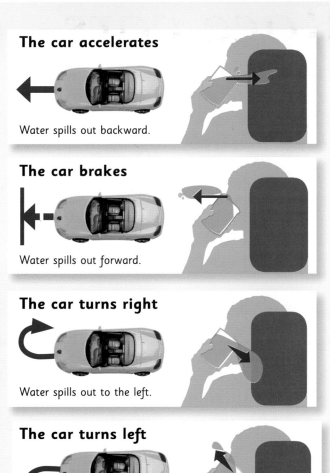

The car accelerates

Water spills out backward.

The car brakes

Water spills out forward.

The car turns right

Water spills out to the left.

The car turns left

Water spills out to the right.

This driver's helmet is attached to his seat to stop his head from swinging around because of g-force.

Inertia

G-force is caused by inertia. The law of inertia says that moving objects try to travel straight at a constant speed. When a car stops abruptly, your body tries to keep going forward.

Steering wheel

Because an F1 driver is concentrating so hard on winning a race and because the space he is in is so tight, all the controls for the car are on hand on his steering wheel. He has just two foot pedals—the brake and the accelerator.

These buttons fulfill all the driver's needs, from traction control to drinks dispenser—drinks are pumped by tube straight into the driver's mouth. He doesn't worry about spilling HIS drink!

Including the driver, the minimum weight is 1,300 lb (600 kg).

Up to speed

Once you're on the move, you naturally want to go as fast as you can. But what makes sports cars really fast and tankers really slow? Speed isn't just about raw power—other factors are at work.

Acceleration isn't just speeding up. Scientists also use it to describe all changes in velocity, like slowing down and even changing direction.

Speed, velocity, and acceleration

You measure speed by dividing the distance traveled by the time it takes. Speed is not the same as velocity, which is a measure of how fast you are going in a particular direction. You feel acceleration when you pedal your bike really hard. Acceleration measures how quickly your velocity is changing.

Horsepower?

Engine power is still measured using a very old unit—the horsepower. It is based on how many horses would be needed to provide the same amount of pulling power. An average mid-sized car is equivalent to 135 horses.

How fast are electric cars?

Pulling power

If you have a powerful engine you can accelerate very fast, which is why a sports car will always beat a lawnmower. But if you give a ride to an elephant your acceleration will suffer. That is because it takes more force to speed up heavy objects.

Milk tanker vs. Ariel Atom

Both have a 300 horsepower engine. A full tanker can weigh as much as 110 tons (100 metric tons). The Atom weighs half a ton. Even though they have the same pulling power, the weight of the milk means the tanker takes 35 seconds to accelerate from 0 to 60 mph (97 km/h). The Atom can do it in 2.7 seconds, making it one of the fastest accelerating road cars in the world.

Not such a drag

Nothing accelerates as fast as a dragster—not even the space shuttle. Dragsters can go from 0 to 330 mph (530 km/h) in less than 4.5 seconds. They use nitromethane as fuel, which provides twice as much power as gas. The rear wheels have to be really big to transfer the high power made by the engine.

Superfast cars
If you want to go really fast and break records, then there's only one solution—strap a jet engine or two to your chassis. Jet engines don't use pistons. Instead, they suck air through the front of the engine, use it to burn fuel, and then blast the hot exhaust out of the back. This pushes the car forward at speeds of up to 760 mph (1,230 km/h).

The Tesla Roadster can reach speeds of 130 mph (210 km/h).

Powering up

Most cars are powered by gasoline engines, but there are many other ways to power a vehicle. In the future, renewable forms of power that don't depend on fossil fuels such as gasoline will become more important.

Electric car

Electric cars carry energy in rechargeable batteries instead of gas. The battery releases energy as electricity, which drives a motor that turns the wheels. One problem is that recharging can take hours.

Solar car

The solar panels on a solar car use sunlight to generate electricity. The electricity powers an electric motor that turns the wheels. Solar cars are not powerful and so must be very light and streamlined.

Solar cars work best in very sunny places. They tend to be flat and very wide or long to create room for the large solar panels on the roof.

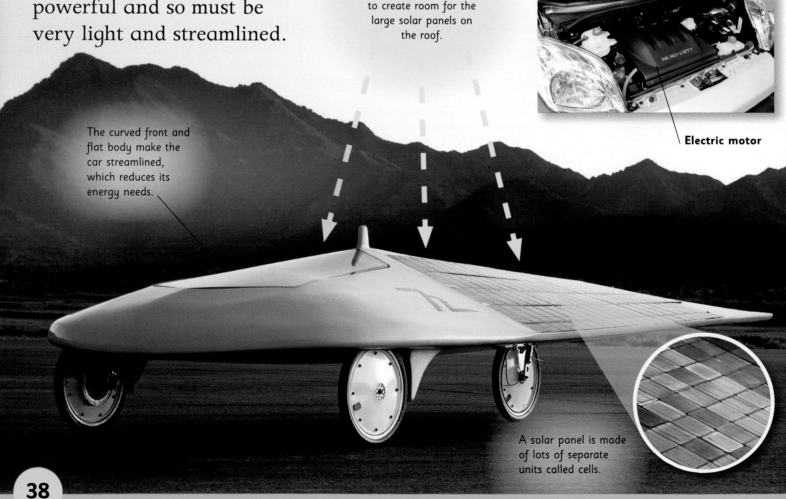

The curved front and flat body make the car streamlined, which reduces its energy needs.

Electric motor

A solar panel is made of lots of separate units called cells.

When did the hybrid car go on sale?

Biofuel

Many ordinary cars can run on biofuels—fuels made from plants. Biodiesel, for instance, is a biofuel made from vegetable oil. In some countries, including Brazil and the US, gasoline is diluted with alcohol made from corn or sugarcane. Using biofuels reduces pollution, but biofuels can harm the environment because growing them uses vast areas of land.

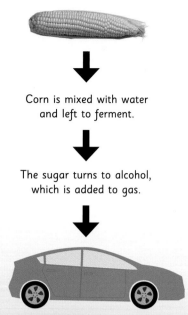

Corn is mixed with water and left to ferment.

The sugar turns to alcohol, which is added to gas.

Hydrogen power

Hydrogen-powered vehicles use liquid hydrogen as a fuel instead of gasoline. The hydrogen flows into a device called a fuel cell, which combines hydrogen with oxygen from the air to make water and electricity. The electricity drives the car's motor and wheels, just as in an electric car.

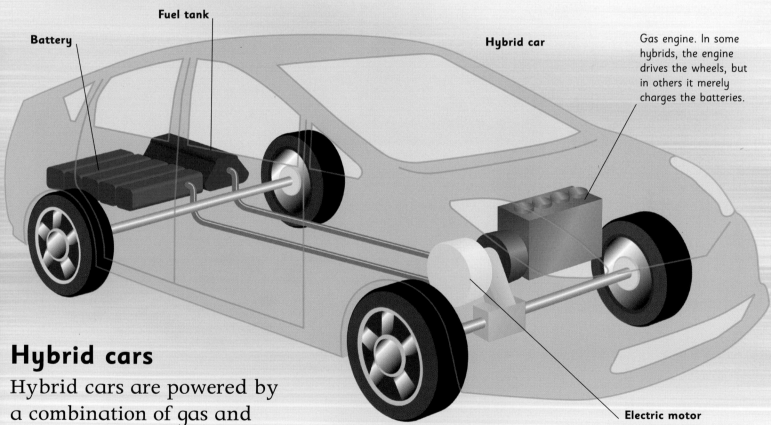

Battery

Fuel tank

Hybrid car

Gas engine. In some hybrids, the engine drives the wheels, but in others it merely charges the batteries.

Electric motor

Hybrid cars

Hybrid cars are powered by a combination of gas and electricity from batteries. When the car stops, the brakes capture energy and use it to charge the batteries. A computer switches between the two forms of power to make the best use of energy.

Air car

The air car works a bit like a balloon. High pressure air is stored in an air tank and released through a valve when the driver pushes the accelerator. The jet of air turns the engine.

In 1917.

Trains and tracks

Most countries have a railroad system where trains travel on steel tracks. Trains are often powered by electricity that runs through rails or cables.

This train's cars tilt to help it travel around corners at high speed.

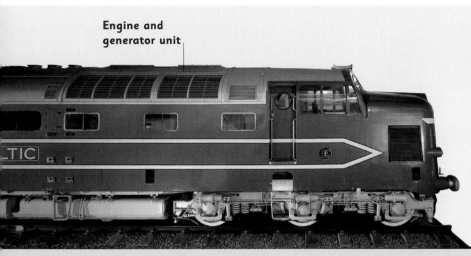

Engine and generator unit

Diesel electric

Some electric trains run on diesel fuel. The diesel is burned to make electricity. This electricity powers the motors that make the wheels turn and the train move.

Most freight trains are powered by diesel electrics.

Electric third rail

Other trains use an electrified third rail. The train picks up the electricity using a device called a shoe.

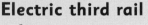

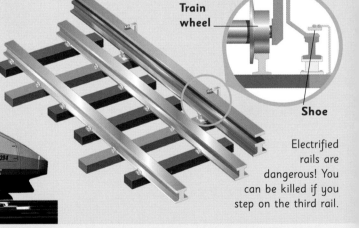

Train wheel

Shoe

Electrified rails are dangerous! You can be killed if you step on the third rail.

Overhead cables

There are trains that take electricity from overhead cables using a metal arm. The cables carry high-voltage electricity—around 25,000 volts.

The train's metal arm is called a pantograph.

What color lights do signals use?

Signals

Signals tell the train driver when it is safe to move forward, when to proceed carefully to the next section of track, and when to stop.

You need wheels

Trains have metal wheels with a rim, called a flange, on the inside to stop them slipping off the track. Usually the flanges never touch the rails, but if they do you hear a squealing noise.

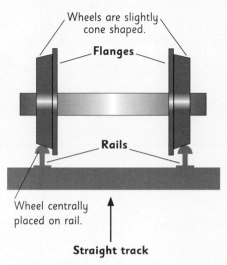

Wheels are slightly cone shaped.

Flanges

Rails

Wheel centrally placed on rail.

Straight track

On the tracks

Railroad tracks guide trains from station to station. They are made of steel and usually welded together to give a smooth ride. Some rails are moveable. These are called points. They help the train switch from one track to another.

A

B

Points

C

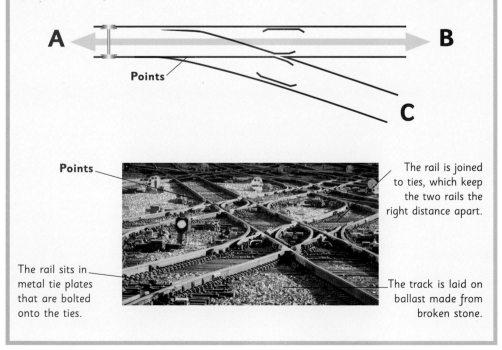

Points

The rail is joined to ties, which keep the two rails the right distance apart.

The rail sits in metal tie plates that are bolted onto the ties.

The track is laid on ballast made from broken stone.

Train travel

Trains are the most efficient way to move people and goods.

Freight trains carry goods and can be more than 4 miles (7 km) long.

Bullet trains in Japan provided the world's first high-speed rail service.

The French TGV is the fastest train ever built. It can go at 322 mph (515 km/h).

Eurostar travels between England and France through the Channel Tunnel.

The Trans-Siberian Express makes the longest trip— 5,857 miles (9,297 km).

The Qinghai–Tibet railroad is the highest anywhere—passengers need to carry oxygen.

Brakes

Metal wheels can slip when the train engineer brakes on icy rails. So a small amount of sand is dropped in front of them to help them grip the rail.

Red, yellow, and green, like traffic lights.

Gases and liquids

Air and water are important examples of two types of substance—liquids and gases. They behave in different ways.

What's a molecule?

Liquids and gases are made of molecules. Molecules are so tiny you can't see them with the naked eye. Molecules are made of even tinier particles called atoms. Everything in the universe is made from atoms.

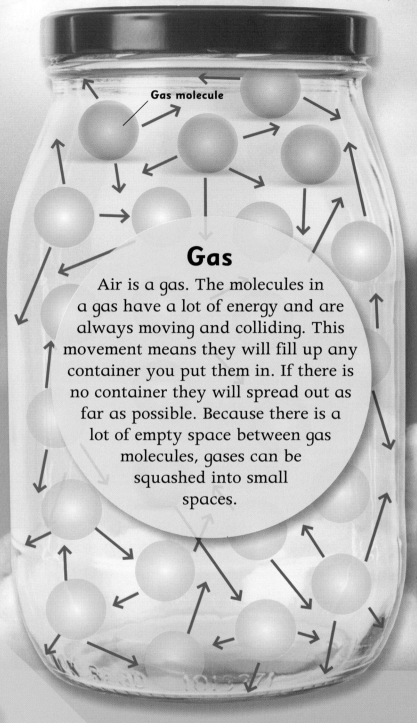

Gas molecule

Gas

Air is a gas. The molecules in a gas have a lot of energy and are always moving and colliding. This movement means they will fill up any container you put them in. If there is no container they will spread out as far as possible. Because there is a lot of empty space between gas molecules, gases can be squashed into small spaces.

Feel the breeze

You can feel air molecules moving when the wind blows. Wind is simply air molecules being pushed by a force we call pressure.

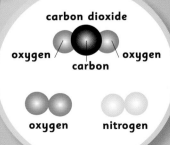

carbon dioxide

oxygen — carbon — oxygen

oxygen

nitrogen

Air molecules

Air is made up of lots of different atoms bonded together in groups called molecules. The main molecules in air are nitrogen, oxygen, and carbon dioxide.

What do we call materials in which the atoms cannot move?

Scientists call water molecules H_2O (H stands for hydrogen and O stands for oxygen).

Liquid

Liquids always take on the shape of their container. The molecules in a liquid are closer together than in a gas, but have less energy to move around. Special forces hold the liquid molecules together. It is very difficult to squash a liquid into a smaller space.

Water molecule

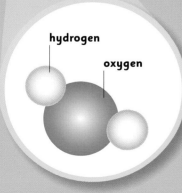

hydrogen

oxygen

Water molecules

Water molecules are made of two hydrogen atoms bonded to one oxygen atom. Water molecules are so sticky they clump together to form drops.

Look through the "Gases and liquids" pages and see if you can identify the picture clues below.

Become an expert...

on how ships float, 46–47

on how airplanes fly, 52–53

43

Solids.

How fluids work

Gases (such as air) and liquids (such as water) are known as "fluids." This is because they move in a similar way and can flow around corners and fill containers.

Streamlined car
A car is designed to be as streamlined as possible, so air can pass over it smoothly.

Fluid motion

Fluids flow smoothly over curved (streamlined) objects. They do not flow smoothly over shapes that have corners and bumps. These slow fluids down, causing a force called drag.

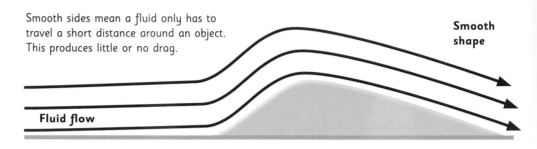

Smooth sides mean a fluid only has to travel a short distance around an object. This produces little or no drag.

Smooth shape

Fluid flow

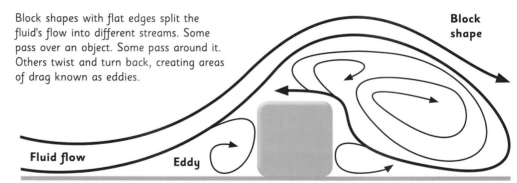

Block shapes with flat edges split the fluid's flow into different streams. Some pass over an object. Some pass around it. Others twist and turn back, creating areas of drag known as eddies.

Block shape

Fluid flow   Eddy

Sir Isaac Newton discovered gravity when an apple fell from a tree.

Gravity and weight

Gravity is the force that keeps you stuck to the ground. It also keeps the Moon in orbit around the Earth, and keeps the Earth traveling around the Sun. Gravity gives everything weight. Without it you would simply float away as if you were in space.

What is more dense—water or air?

How dense?

The weight of an object also depends on its mass—the amount of tiny particles (called atoms) it contains. Some substances pack more atoms into a space than others. The more closely packed the atoms are, the more dense the substance is. All substances have different densities.

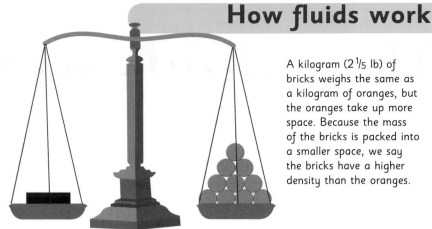

A kilogram (2⅕ lb) of bricks weighs the same as a kilogram of oranges, but the oranges take up more space. Because the mass of the bricks is packed into a smaller space, we say the bricks have a higher density than the oranges.

Moving through fluids

When objects move through a fluid they either float or sink, depending on their density.

An object will **float** in air if it is **less dense** than air.

The gas inside the balloon is lighter than the air around it, so it rises slowly.

An object will **sink** in air if it is **more dense** than air.

Apples are denser than air so they drop from trees.

An object will **float** in water if it is **less dense** than water.

Boats float because they are mainly filled with air, which is less dense than water.

An object will **sink** in water if it is **more dense** than water.

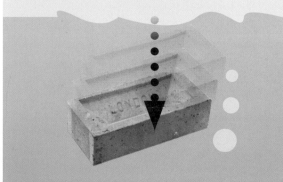

Brick molecules are very close together, making bricks dense, so they sink.

Water is 1,000 times more dense than air.

Float that boat

How do ships float, and why do they sometimes sink? It's all about buoyancy.

Setting sail

A ship is very heavy, especially when it's loaded with crew, passengers, and cargo. But the ship still floats because as it pushes down, it displaces water, and the displaced water pushes upward. If the ship weighs less than the displaced water, it will float. (See page 45.)

Floating beach ball

Buoyancy

When an object weighs less than the amount of water it displaces, it floats (or is "buoyant"). If it weighs more, it sinks.

Sinking golf ball

The weight of the ship is spread out across the hull.

Gravity

Buoyancy

Balancing act

While buoyancy pushes the boat upward, gravity pulls it downward. These two forces balance each other out, so a ship can float on the water.

What's the longest ship in the world?

Safety systems

A ship may sink if it takes on water. To prevent this, ships have safety features such as bulkheads—walls that divide large areas into smaller ones.

If one compartment starts to leak, the bulkheads stop the water from flooding the ship.

Bulkheads

Double hull

A big ship usually has a double hull, which is like a tire with an inner tube. It gives extra protection if the ship collides with rocks or icebergs.

Hull   Double hull

The steel hull is full of air, which is very light and keeps the ship afloat.

That sinking feeling

The air inside a ship's hull makes the ship less dense than the water around it. If the ship hits a rock and rips a hole in its hull, water pours in and replaces the air. This makes the ship more dense and it sinks.

This ship is taking on water and has started to sink.

Going down

Submarines are not like other boats— they have to be able to sink or float on command. They do this by filling and emptying their ballast tanks with air or water.

1 The weight of a submarine's hull helps it to sink, but it can't sink when there is air in the ballast tanks. Most of the air is let out through a valve. Some air is compressed (squashed) into a small holding tank. Water is then pumped into the tanks and the sub sinks.

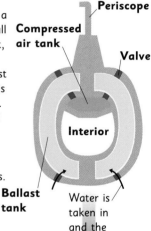

Periscope

Compressed air tank

Valve

Interior

Ballast tank

Water is taken in and the sub sinks.

Air flows into the ballast tanks.

2 When the sub is underwater, air is pumped back into the ballast tanks until the density of the sub matches that of the water around it. The sub can stay at one level as it moves through the water.

Water is forced out.

3 When it's time to surface, more air is pumped into the tanks, pushing the water out. Once it's at the surface, air is sucked in to fill the ballast tanks and the sub floats.

Air fills the tanks and the sub rises.

Water is forced out.

An oil tanker called *Knock Nevis*. It's 1,504 ft (458.4 m) long.

Floating balloons

Why do some balloons rise up into the air and others drop to the floor? To understand this you have to look at the gases inside them.

An airship can rise over 6,500 feet (2,000 meters). That's lower than an airplane's usual cruising height of 29,000 feet (8,800 meters).

Party balloons are filled with helium gas.

Helium
This balloon is filled with a gas called helium. Helium is lighter than air, so this balloon floats.

At parties, helium balloons are tied down so they don't float off!

Heavy air
When a balloon is filled with a gas that is lighter than air it floats. When it is filled with a gas that is heavier than air, it sinks.

Carbon dioxide
When you breathe out (into a balloon) the air contains more carbon dioxide than normal air, making it heavier. So a balloon you blow up with your breath will sink.

Helium facts

Helium gas has no smell. It makes up about 7 percent of natural gas.

Deep-sea divers breathe in a mixture of helium and oxygen.

Helium boils at a very low temperature, -452°F (-269°C), and turns to gas.

Helium, found in stars, is named after the Greek word for the Sun—helios.

Liquid helium is colorless, and very cold. It helps launch space rockets.

What is the only element to be discovered in space before it was found on Earth?

Floating balloons

Flying ships of air

An airship is known as a lighter-than-air (LTA) craft. Airships have a main helium-filled balloon and two other large internal balloons called ballonets. To control how high an airship floats, the ballonets take in or release air.

How airships rise and fall

Airship rising

Helium

Ballonets deflate to go higher

Air expelled through air valves

To rise, the ballonets are closed and deflated. The helium makes the airship float upward.

Airship falling

Air inflating ballonets

Air taken in filling the ballonets

To descend back down to Earth, the ballonets are filled with the heavier air, making the airship sink.

MERIQUEST

How hot-air balloons work

Hot-air balloons float upward when the air inside them is heated. This gives the air molecules more energy and they move farther apart, which makes the air lighter.

 Cold air weighs more because its molecules are closer together.

 Hot air is lighter because its molecules are farther apart.

The balloon holds the hot air. Its shape makes it hard for the hot air to escape.

A flap at the top of the balloon allows hot air to escape and controls how quickly the balloon sinks.

Fabric panels are sewn together sideways and lengthwise to give the balloon strength.

Skirt

Propane tanks

Burners use propane gas to produce a hot flame, which heats the air inside the balloon.

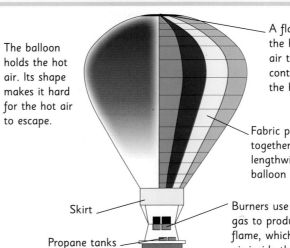

Roller coaster

These rip-roaring rides are powered by gravity itself. They slingshot thrill-seeking passengers along at breathtaking speeds.

Some older roller coasters run on intricate wooden scaffolding.

Going up...

As the roller coaster goes up the first, tallest hill (called the lift hill), it's gradually building up potential energy.

There is maximum potential energy at the top of the hill.

Over the top

At the top of a hill, roller-coaster cars have high potential energy. This becomes kinetic energy as the roller coaster rolls down the slope.

arghhh

The cars gain speed as they roll down the hill.

Rushing down a steep slope can make you feel almost weightless, which may be quite uncomfortable!

Chain reaction

Roller-coaster cars don't have motors. They're pulled to the top of the first hill by a chain connected to a motor at the top.

Where was the world's first roller coaster?

Wheeeeeeee!
Lots of different things affect the way you feel when you're whizzing around a roller coaster.

➡ **Acceleration force**
➡ **Apparent weight**
➡ **Gravity (weight)**

Shoulder harness

Flexible metal
The tracks and supports of most roller coasters are made from hollow steel. This can be shaped into loops and corkscrews.

Safety first
All riders are protected by a safety harness. Brakes are built into the track, not the cars— they are used at the end of the ride, or in emergencies.

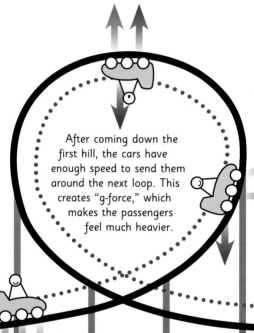

After coming down the first hill, the cars have enough speed to send them around the next loop. This creates "g-force," which makes the passengers feel much heavier.

There is maximum kinetic energy at the bottom of the hill.

Cars lose momentum throughout the ride, so the hills have to get smaller.

Focus the force
The roller coaster track acts as a channel for gravity. When the track slopes down, the car fronts go faster—when it tilts up, the car backs are pulled down, and they go slower.

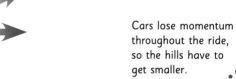

— Steel track
— Load wheels
— Guide wheels
— Upstop wheels

Roller-coaster cars are clamped securely to the rails by three sets of wheels.

Ultimate experience
Thrill seekers in Florida can enjoy the new Rip Ride Rockit roller coaster. It's very short and powerful, so it can pivot like a skateboard and climb straight uphill.

Passengers can choose the music they hear while they're terrified.

The very first coaster was an elaborate ice slide built in Russia during the 1600s.

How do planes fly?

Huge, heavy machines seem to defy gravity by staying up in the air! Yet airplanes fly around the world every day. It's because they can create the forces they need to fly.

The forces of flight

"Aerodynamics" means "the way air moves." There are four aerodynamic forces—thrust and drag, and lift and weight. Airplanes need to balance them out in order to fly.

Thrusting forward

Planes need to create thrust to balance out drag. This plane has a propeller to create thrust. As the propeller turns, it draws air past the blades, pulling the plane forward.

Cockpit

Engine

Thrust

Propeller

A bumpy ride

Just like boats bounce over waves, planes can bounce up and down in the air. Called turbulence, this happens when pockets of air move at different speeds. It can be caused by strong winds, storms, or when cold and warm air meet.

Level of plane

Cooler air

Warmer air rises faster, "bumping" the plane upward

The biggest jumbo

The world's largest plane is the Airbus A380. At 239½ ft (73 m) long, this jumbo jet can carry up to 853 passengers. It's 10 times longer than the four-seater Cessna 400.

Cessna 400

Airbus A380

What was the first airplane to stay up in the air successfully?

Lifting up
Lift is the opposite force to weight. A plane creates most of its lift with its wings.

As the plane moves, air flows over its wings. The top of the wing is curved, making the air above the wing move faster than the air under the wing.

Lift

The slow-moving air under the wing pushes up more than the fast-moving air above the wing pushes down. This creates lift.

Airflow

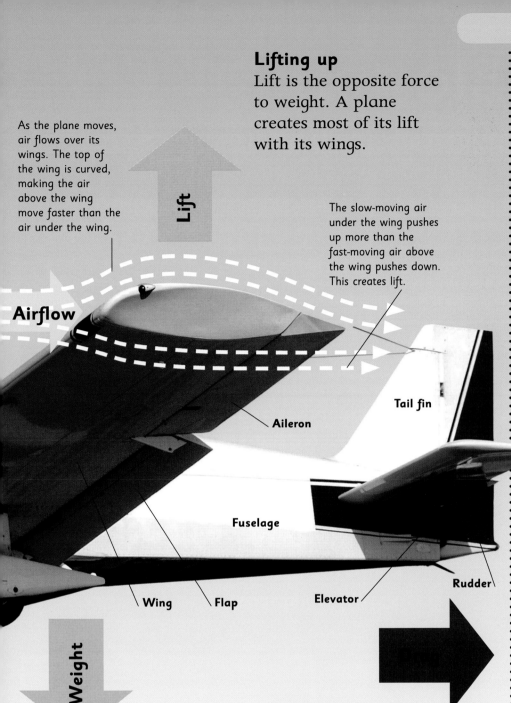

Tail fin

Aileron

Fuselage

Rudder

Wing   Flap

Elevator

Weight

Weighing down
Weight is caused by gravity pulling down on an object. Everything has weight, even air. The Airbus A380 needs to create a lot of lift to balance out its weight—it's a whopping 617 tons (560 metric tons).

Dragging back
Drag is the opposite force from thrust—it slows things down. Imagine trailing your hand in water as you sail along in a boat. You can feel the water push back, or drag, against your hand. Air has the same effect on planes (and anything else that moves). A plane's smooth surface and streamlined shape help to reduce drag.

What does that part do?
Every part of a plane has a job to do, from the streamlined nose to the tail fin that keeps the plane steady in the sky.

Flaps that come down from the wings are used to increase lift during takeoff and landing.

Ailerons on the back edge of the wings are used to "roll" the plane, to make it turn or keep it level.

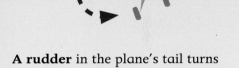

A rudder in the plane's tail turns the plane left or right.

Elevators in the tail move up and down to balance the position of the nose, keeping the plane level.

The *Wright Flyer* On its first outing in 1903, it flew for 12 seconds!

Blastoff!

Space is the final frontier. So far, man has explored only a tiny part of our galaxy, and this has been very difficult, dangerous, and expensive to do.

What makes rockets go?

Most rockets need two different chemicals: a fuel and an oxidizer. When they're mixed together, they cause a fierce but smooth burn—this is funneled downward, propelling the rocket up. Clamps hold it down while the power builds, so it doesn't go end over end and crash. At the word "blastoff," the clamps are removed and the rocket is on its way. Good luck!

Nose cone

Command module

Service module

Rocket stage containing lunar module

Instrument unit

Rocket stage containing fuel

Engine

Rocket stage containing fuel

Engines

Rocket stage

Thrust

Gravity

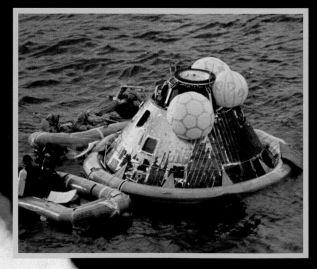

When the Apollo lunar-mission crew returned to Earth, they landed in the Pacific Ocean and were rescued by Navy personnel.

When was the first liquid-fueled rocket made?

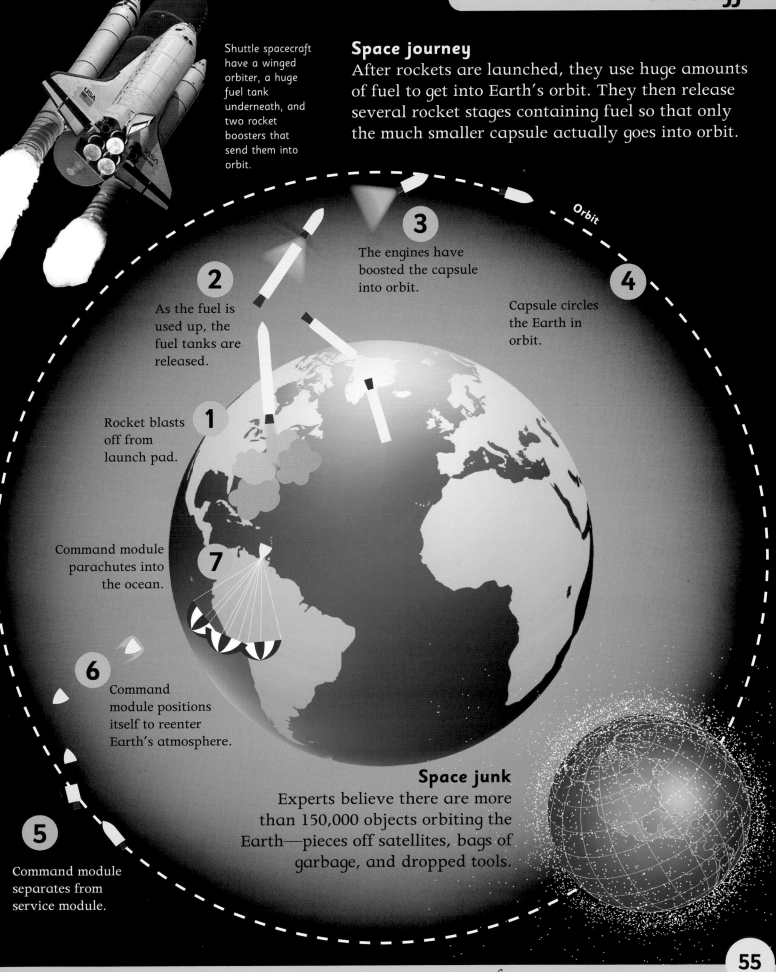

Shuttle spacecraft have a winged orbiter, a huge fuel tank underneath, and two rocket boosters that send them into orbit.

Space journey
After rockets are launched, they use huge amounts of fuel to get into Earth's orbit. They then release several rocket stages containing fuel so that only the much smaller capsule actually goes into orbit.

Orbit

3
The engines have boosted the capsule into orbit.

2
As the fuel is used up, the fuel tanks are released.

4
Capsule circles the Earth in orbit.

1
Rocket blasts off from launch pad.

Command module parachutes into the ocean.

7

6
Command module positions itself to reenter Earth's atmosphere.

Space junk
Experts believe there are more than 150,000 objects orbiting the Earth—pieces off satellites, bags of garbage, and dropped tools.

5
Command module separates from service module.

March 1926, by Dr. Robert H. Goddard in Massachusetts.

What is energy?

Energy is what makes everything happen. It is involved in every action that we make. It powers your muscles, runs your car, and lights your home. Without energy you could not ride a bike, watch television, or fly in an airplane.

Different types of energy

Energy can't be made, just changed from one type to another. Here are some of the main types.

Light

is a form of energy that we can see. Most of the energy on Earth comes from the Sun as light.

Heat energy

is the energy of atoms or molecules vibrating. The hotter an object gets, the faster and more violently the atoms or molecules vibrate.

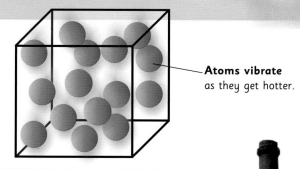

Atoms vibrate
as they get hotter.

Nuclear energy

is stored in atoms. Nuclear energy is used to run power plants that generate electricity.

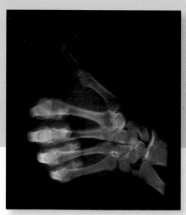

Electromagnetic energy
is carried by X-rays, radio waves, and microwaves.

56

Everything is made up of atoms—but what are they?

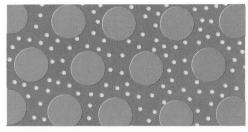

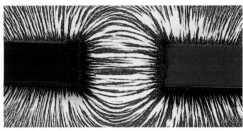

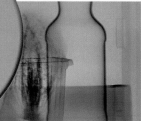

Curiosity quiz

Look through the "What is energy?" pages and see if you can identify the picture clues below.

Gravitational energy

is the stored energy in an object that has been lifted but is not allowed to fall. Dams can turn gravitational energy into electrical energy.

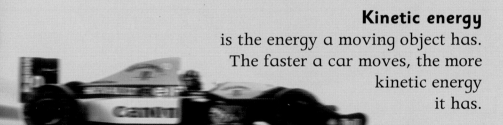

Kinetic energy

is the energy a moving object has. The faster a car moves, the more kinetic energy it has.

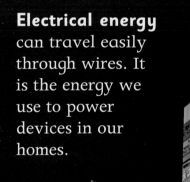

Electrical energy

can travel easily through wires. It is the energy we use to power devices in our homes.

Become an expert...

on power plants, pages 62–63

on gravity, pages 44–45

The smallest particles that something can be broken down into.

It's electric!

If you flip a switch to make something work, it probably runs on electricity. Most of the energy we use every day is electric.

What is electricity?

This magical power source comes from electrons—tiny charged particles on the outside of atoms. They move from atom to atom creating electrical energy, and this energy travels on a circuit.

Starting small

To understand electricity, you have to look at the teeny tiny building blocks that everything is made from—atoms.

weird or what?

Electrical energy travels very quickly, at 125,000 miles (200,000 km) per second. That's two-thirds as fast as the fastest thing ever—light!

Plugs have metal prongs that connect with the power supply wired into the wall.

Electric sockets are live. You should never put your finger or an object (other than a plug) into a socket—you might get an electric shock.

Electricity passes freely from the socket to the lamp through the wiring.

Electrons carry an electrical charge.

Atom

Electrons

Electricity flows this way

Electricity is passed along wires by electrons. When you supply energy to the wire, it makes the electrons move along it, carrying electric charge with them.

When you switch on a lamp, electric current flows along the flex to the bulb, lighting it up.

58

Simple circuit

A flashlight works using a simple electrical circuit. Batteries produce electricity, which flows around the circuit to power the bulb so it lights up.

Lamp filament

When the switch is on "off," the circuit is broken and the bulb goes out.

Broken circuit

Off

To turn off the flashlight the circuit is broken.

On

Slide switch

When the switch slides to "on," the circuit is complete and current flows all the way to the bulb, which lights up.

Off

Plastic case

Batteries

Metal switch contacts

Metal spring

Electricity flows from the batteries and along the metal wire.

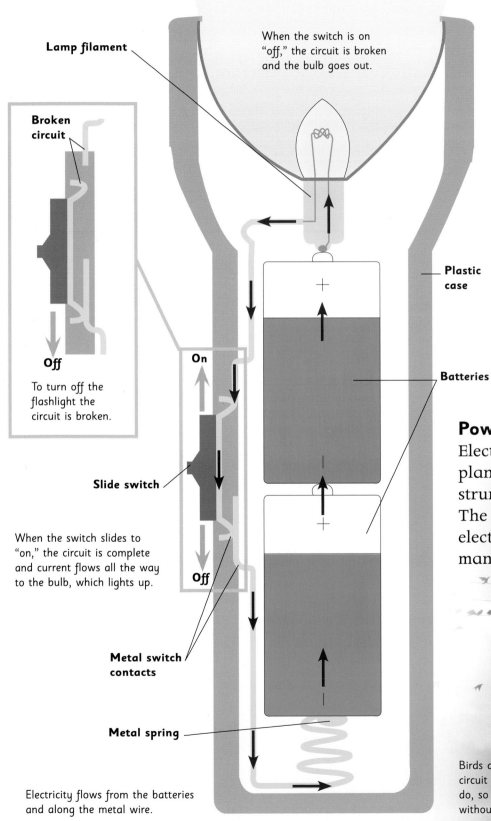

Electricity

When we talk about electricity, we use the same words over and over again.

 Conductor—a material that allows electricity to flow through it easily.

 Circuit—a path that an electrical current can flow along.

 Voltage—a measure of electrical strength.

 Ampere—a basic unit of electrical current.

 Current—a flow of electricity through a conductor.

Power masts

Electricity travels from power plants along thick cables often strung between big metal towers. The cables carry very high levels of electricity—enough to kill an adult man if they fell on him.

Birds don't complete an electrical circuit with the ground like people do, so they can sit on cables without being harmed.

An Italian named Alessandro Volta made the first battery in 1800.

The power of magnets

Magnets create an invisible force known as magnetism that repels and attracts certain substances, like iron. Electricity and magnetism have a close relationship.

BEWARE: ELECTRICAL CHARGE!

Can you field the force?

A magnetic field is the space around a magnet where its force can be felt. The force gets weaker as the field gets farther from the magnet. It is strongest at the two poles.

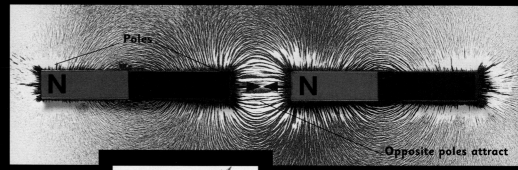

Iron filings reveal the magnetic field around a magnet

Poles

Opposite poles attract

Similar poles repel

Magnets have two points where their field is strongest, known as poles. Each magnet has a north and south pole. These can attract and repel other magnets. Similar poles repel and opposites attract.

Magnetic Earth

The Earth acts like a gigantic magnet. It has a magnetic north and south pole, although they aren't in the same place as the geographical poles, but are very close. Over the Earth's lifetime the magnetic poles have switched around a few times.

Super magnets

These are really sticky magnets. They can be natural magnets or electromagnets.

The maglev train uses an electromagnet.

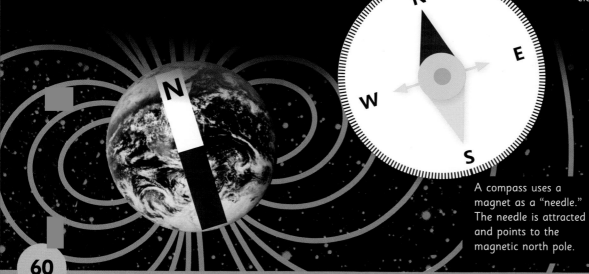

A compass uses a magnet as a "needle." The needle is attracted and points to the magnetic north pole.

Which elements are attracted to magnets?

Electromagnets

A magnet can produce electricity and electricity can create magnetism. An iron bar can become magnetic when an electric wire is wound around it in a coil. A moving magnet can also make an electric current in a coil of wire. Electromagnetic generators are used to create electricity at power plants.

Everyday magnets

Magnets are used in many everyday items, such as:

Audio speakers use electromagnets to make sound vibrations.

Some handbags close with magnetic clasps.

Credit cards use a magnetic strip to store your information.

Central locking in a car uses a series of electromagnets to lock up.

The wheel has to keep turning for the dynamo to light the bulb.

Wheel power

A simple example of an electromagnetic generator is a bicycle dynamo. It uses the kinetic energy produced by the spinning wheel to turn the magnet past a coil of wire. The movement of the magnetic field produces enough electric current to light a bicycle light.

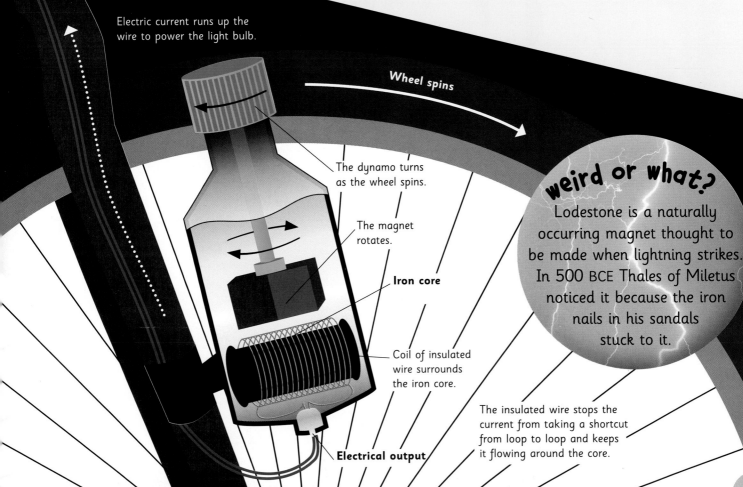

Electric current runs up the wire to power the light bulb.

Wheel spins

The dynamo turns as the wheel spins.

The magnet rotates.

Iron core

Coil of insulated wire surrounds the iron core.

Electrical output

The insulated wire stops the current from taking a shortcut from loop to loop and keeps it flowing around the core.

weird or what?
Lodestone is a naturally occurring magnet thought to be made when lightning strikes. In 500 BCE Thales of Miletus noticed it because the iron nails in his sandals stuck to it.

Iron (Fe), Nickel (Ni), and Cobalt (Co) are all attracted to magnets.

Power plants

There are two kinds of energy—renewable and nonrenewable. Earth will run out of non-renewable fuels, but renewable energy comes from endless resources such as wind and sun.

In Shanghai, China, vast quantities of coal are loaded on a conveyor belt.

Burn, burn, burn

Most power plants burn nonrenewable fossil fuels like coal, oil, and natural gas. These are formed from fossilized plankton or plants that lived millions of years ago. Fossil fuels release energy from these plants when they're burned.

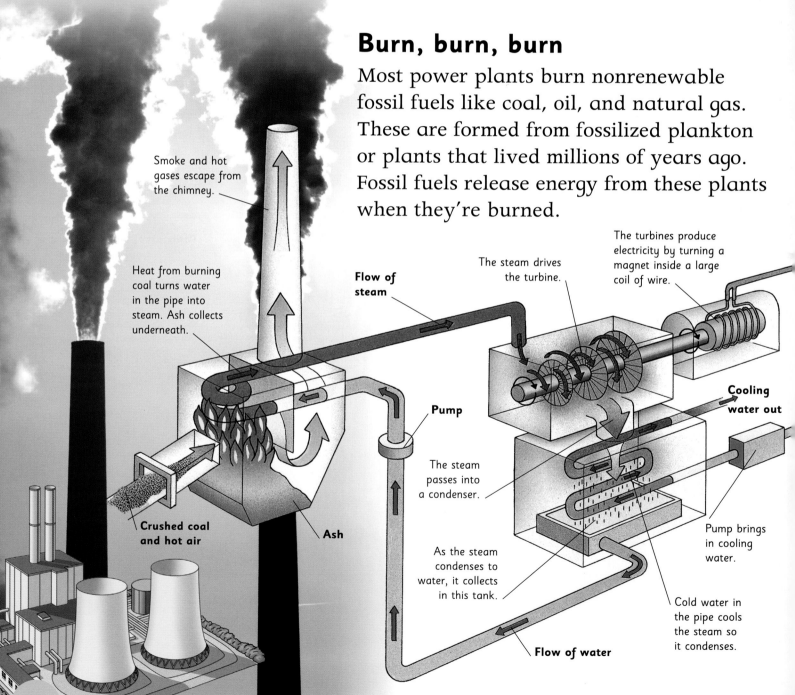

Smoke and hot gases escape from the chimney.

Heat from burning coal turns water in the pipe into steam. Ash collects underneath.

Crushed coal and hot air

Ash

Flow of steam

The steam drives the turbine.

The turbines produce electricity by turning a magnet inside a large coil of wire.

Pump

The steam passes into a condenser.

As the steam condenses to water, it collects in this tank.

Cooling water out

Pump brings in cooling water.

Cold water in the pipe cools the steam so it condenses.

Flow of water

How far does power travel?

Dangerous power

Nuclear power plants create energy by splitting uranium atoms, which release heat to run the generators that make electricity. Nuclear power is nonrenewable because there is a limited supply of nuclear fuels. The waste from these fuels is radioactive, so they may damage cells and cause cancer.

On April 26, 1986, at 1:23 a.m., Reactor Four at Chernobyl Nuclear Power Plant in Ukraine exploded. Over 20 years later, an inspector checks the interior (left).

Become an expert...
on renewable energy, pages **66-67**

Green power

Renewable energy sources will always be there—and they're less harmful to the environment than fossil fuels.

 Solar power comes from the Sun. In theory, it could provide all our energy.

 Hydroelectric power is created by falling water, like a dam or waterfall.

 Wind power is generated by turbines. Lots of them together make a wind farm.

 Tidal power uses water in the form of waves rather than waterfalls.

 Biofuels (like corn oil) are made from growing things, so they're renewable.

 Geothermal power comes from heat deep, deep down toward the Earth's core.

Transformer "steps up" the voltage.

Stretched between towers, cables carry high currents.

Power masts are huge steel towers. They have extra wires running along the top to ground lightning.

Substations reduce voltage and send power in different directions.

Local grid

Electricity is wired to power points in your home. It connects with equipment through a plug.

On the way...

All over the world, rows of masts march across the landscape. They support the high-tension cables that carry electricity from power plants to homes and offices.

Cables below ground

Running out

Most of the energy we use comes from burning fossil fuels. But these fuel sources won't last forever, so we need to start thinking about how we can use less energy, and try to find other ways of providing it.

What can you do to save energy?

Grow your own fruit and vegetables. Try to eat food that is produced locally.

Don't waste heat. Ask your parents to make sure your home is insulated.

Save gasoline. When you can, walk instead of asking for a ride.

Turn off your television and computer. Don't leave them on standby!

Switch off lights when you leave a room, and use energy-saving light bulbs.

Dry laundry outside instead of using a dryer.

Recycle and reuse items such as glass, plastic, and paper.

Steam power

Electricity that comes from coal is relatively inexpensive to make. In a machine called a pulverizer, the coal is broken down into a fine powder, then burned in a furnace. The furnace heats a boiler to produce steam. The steam powers turbines that run generators to create electricity.

Turbines in a coal-fired power plant without their metal covers.

Oil and gas

We get oil by drilling under the ground—from dry land, or from the ocean floor. Today, we use oil for 38 percent of our energy, either as fuel for heating, or turned into gasoline for cars and planes. Experts think oil reserves will run out in about 40 years.

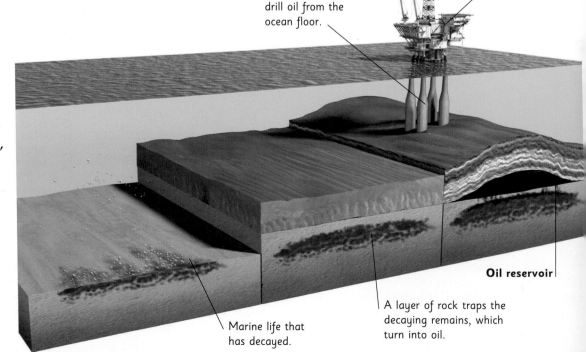
Tall pipes are used to drill oil from the ocean floor.

Oil rig

Marine life that has decayed.

A layer of rock traps the decaying remains, which turn into oil.

Oil reservoir

How much oil can the largest oil rig store?

Peat is the earliest stage in the formation of coal.

Decaying plants form peat.

Compressed peat becomes lignite.

Compressed lignite turns into coal.

weird or what?

In the US, about half of all the electricity used comes from coal-burning power plants.

Underground gas

Natural gas is also a fossil fuel. It comes from coal beds, marshes, bogs, and oil reserves. The largest reserves of natural gas are shared between Iran and Qatar, although Russia is the world's biggest gas producer. Natural gas is likely to run out in about 100 years. At the moment, it provides 23 percent of our energy.

Black diamonds

Like diamonds, coal is a form of carbon. Excavated from the ground through deep mines or open pits, it provides 25 percent of the world's energy supply. If we continue digging coal at the current rate, we have about a 250 years' supply left in the Earth.

Gas facts

Easily piped into homes, natural gas is completely clear and odorless. When it burns, it releases lots of energy, which makes it suitable for use in cooking, heating, and cooling. It also gives off fewer harmful substances than other fossil fuels, so it's slightly greener.

The Hibernia platform in the Atlantic Ocean can hold 1.3 million barrels of crude oil.

Renewable energy

Energy made from fossil fuels will eventually run out, but certain types of energy are renewable, which means that we can go on using them forever.

Become an expert... on energy-efficient homes, 72–73

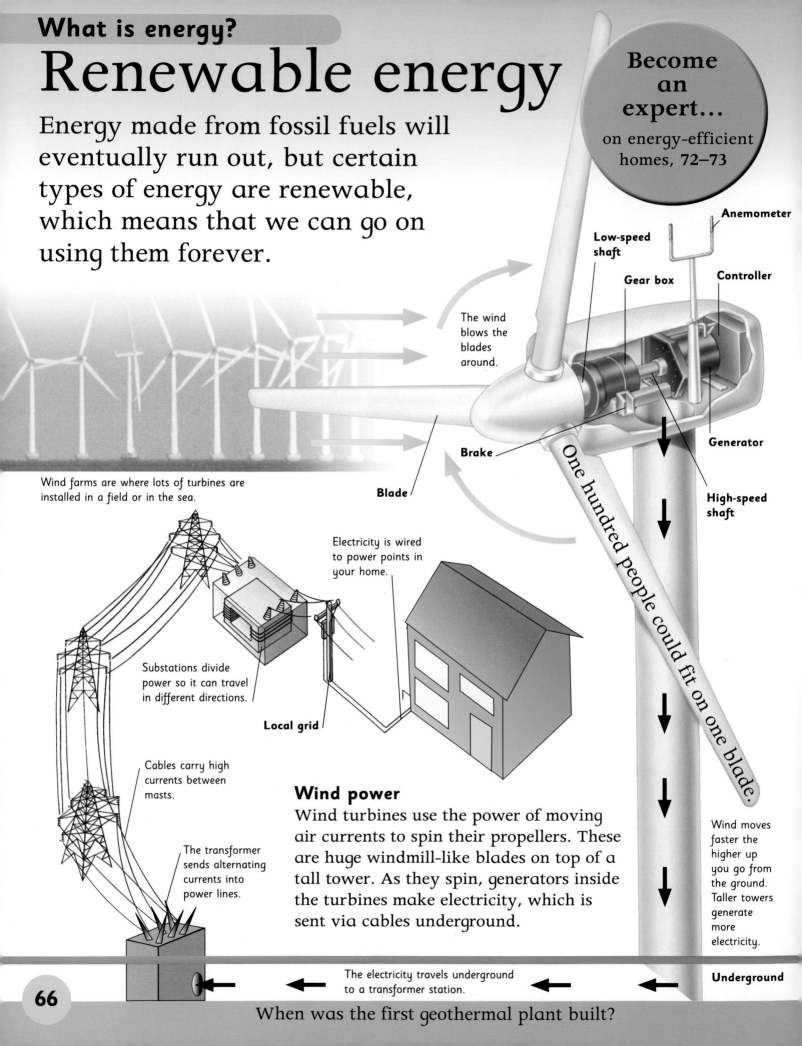

Anemometer

Low-speed shaft

Gear box

Controller

The wind blows the blades around.

Generator

Brake

High-speed shaft

Blade

One hundred people could fit on one blade.

Wind farms are where lots of turbines are installed in a field or in the sea.

Electricity is wired to power points in your home.

Substations divide power so it can travel in different directions.

Local grid

Cables carry high currents between masts.

The transformer sends alternating currents into power lines.

Wind power

Wind turbines use the power of moving air currents to spin their propellers. These are huge windmill-like blades on top of a tall tower. As they spin, generators inside the turbines make electricity, which is sent via cables underground.

Wind moves faster the higher up you go from the ground. Taller towers generate more electricity.

The electricity travels underground to a transformer station.

Underground

When was the first geothermal plant built?

Hydroelectric power

A fifth of the world's electricity comes from hydroelectric power plants. Usually a dam is built to trap a river and create a lake. Water is released at a controlled rate and allowed to flow through a spinning machine called a turbine, which drives an electricity generator.

The spillway of a dam is used to control the flow of water.

Water from a reservoir flows down a pipe to a turbine.

Electricity generator

Turbine

Solar energy

Huge glass panels are put on the roofs of buildings to capture energy from the Sun and convert it into electricity. The stronger the sunlight, the more electricity they make.

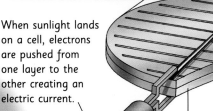

When sunlight lands on a cell, electrons are pushed from one layer to the other creating an electric current.

Solar panel

Photovoltaic cell

Pure silicon doesn't conduct electricity well. Each cell contains silicon doped (made impure) with phosphorus, which produces free electrons.

Silicon doped with boron makes "holes" where electrons are missing in the cell.

Geothermal energy

The Earth's crust is a hot place! Some rocks can be as hot as 1,800 °F (1,000 °C). Geothermal energy uses the heat from these rocks to generate electricity and heat water.

One of the biggest geothermal areas in the world is Iceland. People can swim next door to this geothermal plant in Iceland since the water is so warm.

Biofuels

Biofuels come from fast-growing crops, such as corn, sugar cane, and palm oil. These fuels can add to or replace fossil fuels such as diesel or gas. Biofuels have been criticized for taking up land that could be used to grow food.

The first plant was built in 1904 in Ladarello, Italy.

What's cooking?

The stove is probably the most important piece of equipment in the kitchen. Without it, you'd have to eat all your food raw.

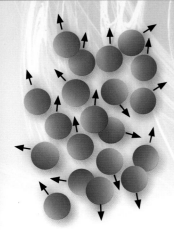

Heat is a form of energy. It comes from the movement of atoms and molecules. The faster the molecules move around, the higher the temperature.

The oven

Inside an electric oven are large coils of wire called heating elements. These heat up when electricity travels through them. They are controlled by a thermostat that keeps the temperature inside constant.

On a burner, the element is in direct contact with the saucepan, which passes the heat through to the food.

Dial controlling the thermostat.

Because the broiler element is much closer to the food and gets hotter than the one in the oven, the food cooks quickly.

Convection ovens have fans that blow air around and keep the whole oven at the same temperature. Food cooks faster in a convection oven.

The oven works by surrounding the food with hot air. Since hot air rises, the top of the oven is slightly hotter than the bottom. When the oven gets too hot, the thermostat turns the heating elements off. It turns them back on again when the oven cools.

Can you cook ice cream in an oven without melting it?

Heat's effect on food

Heat changes food, and different foods react to it differently.
Cooking is simply delicious experiments in chemistry and physics.

Cooking eggs

Egg whites and yolks are made of stringy chains of protein floating in water.

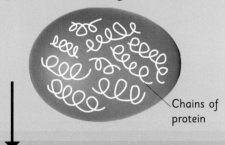

Chains of protein

Each individual chain is twisted and curled up. When you add heat, the chains uncurl and start to link together.

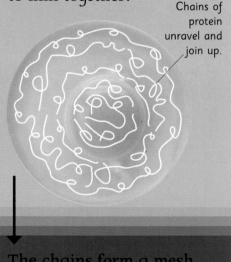

Chains of protein unravel and join up.

The chains form a mesh that traps the water they floated in. The egg is now cooked.

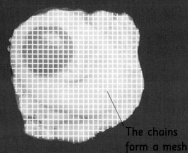

The chains form a mesh.

Baking bread

A basic bread mixture includes flour, water, and yeast. Yeast is a live, single-celled fungus. Flour, when it mixes with water, releases stretchy gluten.

Yeast is inactive until it comes into contact with warm water. When the bread mix is left in a warm place, the yeast starts feeding on the sugars in flour and releases carbon dioxide gas.

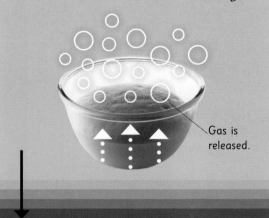

Gas is released.

The gumlike gluten fills with thousands of gas bubbles and the bread rises. Cooking traps the bubbles in the bread.

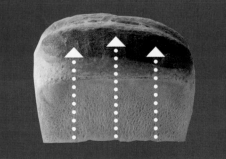

Sweet treats

Many candies are made by simply adding sugar to water and heating the mixture to very high temperatures.

As you cook it, the water boils away, leaving a much stronger solution of sugar. Very strong solutions make toffee or hard tack candy.

Water boils out of the sugar.

If you stir the mixture as it cools, it forms crystals. This is how you make fudge, but you leave hard candy to set without stirring.

Yes, if you make baked Alaska—ice cream covered in meringue!

Keeping cool

We keep food cool so it stays fresh, and we keep liquids cool so they're refreshing to drink. Electricity makes all this possible.

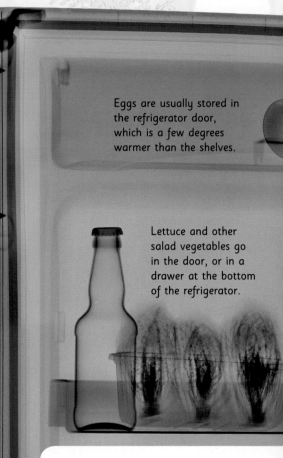

Eggs are usually stored in the refrigerator door, which is a few degrees warmer than the shelves.

Lettuce and other salad vegetables go in the door, or in a drawer at the bottom of the refrigerator.

45°F (7°C) and above

Some foods don't need to be chilled to stay fresh.

Room temperature

Dry foods such as beans and pasta keep very well at room temperature. Root vegetables like potatoes don't need to be refrigerated, but they keep best in a cool place rather than a warm one.

32–45°F (0–7°C)

Let cheese warm up before you eat it.

Refrigerator

The temperature inside a refrigerator is cold enough to slow down the growth of bacteria (germs) in our food, so it stays fresh longer. Dairy products, meat, and fish should always be stored here.

Cool coil

A long coiled pipe is set into the refrigerator walls. Inside is a gas called tetrafluoroethane, which travels around the fridge soaking up heat. This heat travels to a compressor, and is then released at the back, which is why it feels warm there.

Gas coolant circulating around fridge

32°F (0°C) and below

Some treats and desserts are served frozen.

Freezer

Freezers are cold enough to make your skin freeze! Bacteria can't multiply in these temperatures, so food stays fresh for months or even years. Most foods are thawed or warmed before you eat them.

How quickly do bacteria grow at room temperature?

Adjustable temperature control

Warmed coolant

Compressor

Compressor

Control electronics

In just four hours, one bacterium can turn into more than 1,000!

Energy efficiency

Every home needs energy for heating, lighting, cooking, and lots of other things. It's important not to waste this power—not only because you have to pay for it, but also because the sources of this power may one day run out.

Eco living

Sustainable homes are designed to be better for the environment. They have lots of features that save energy and water. They produce fewer carbon emissions and are also cheaper to run.

The outside of the roof is covered in photo-voltaic and solar panels. These generate electricity for the whole house.

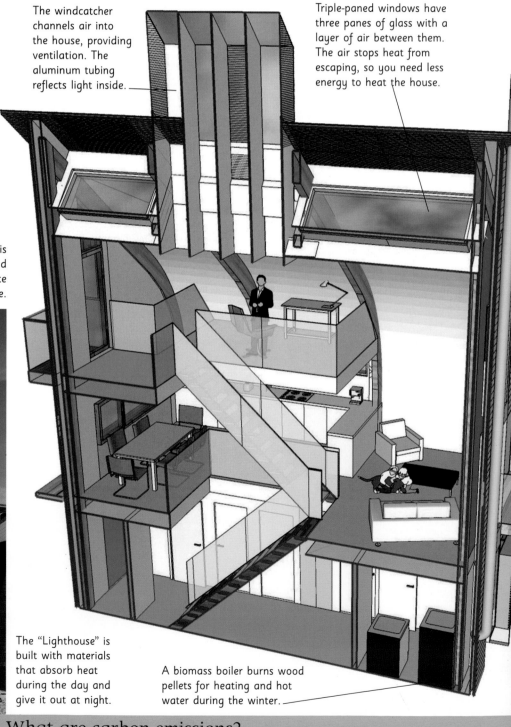

The windcatcher channels air into the house, providing ventilation. The aluminum tubing reflects light inside.

Triple-paned windows have three panes of glass with a layer of air between them. The air stops heat from escaping, so you need less energy to heat the house.

The "Lighthouse" is built with materials that absorb heat during the day and give it out at night.

A biomass boiler burns wood pellets for heating and hot water during the winter.

What are carbon emissions?

In your home

We can all do things to make our homes more energy efficient. A lot of energy is used to heat a house. Ask your parents to lag your attic with insulation to keep heat in. You can also insulate walls and floors, plug gaps around doors and windows, and install double-paned windows.

Thermograms are pictures that show hot things as white and yellow and cold things as blue. The hottest part of this house is its windows, because heat is escaping through them.

When rain hits the roof, it collects in a gutter and runs down a pipe into a recycling tank. The water is used in a washing machine.

Insulating a loft

Become an expert...

on saving energy, pages 64–65

on renewable energy, pages 66–67

When things break...

However energy-efficient you are, electrical goods will eventually wear out. But some items are simply too dangerous to throw away. Old refrigerators contain gases that are harmful if they leak. The safest way to get rid of a broken refrigerator is to contact your local recycling center.

Broken fridges must be taken apart carefully so they don't release harmful gases.

Batteries

Every household uses batteries to power all kinds of things—but batteries eventually run out. So how should you dispose of them?

Change old batteries right away. Batteries contain chemicals that may leak and ruin the gadget.

Don't trash batteries. Recycle them instead—it's better for the environment.

Batteries should never be thrown onto a fire—they might explode.

Make a difference

If you get a new computer or cell phone but there's nothing wrong with the one you had, you can donate the old one to charity. Go online to find charities, schools, and groups that can make good use of your unwanted equipment.

Gases containing carbon that are released into the air and may cause global warming.

Light and sound

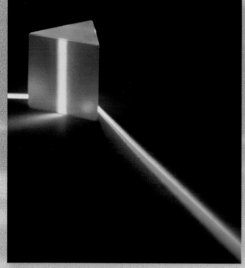

A glass prism splits the light into colors.

Most of what we know about the world we learn by seeing and hearing. Everything we see needs light, and everything we hear involves sound. They can both reach us by traveling in waves.

The Sun's atoms give out lots of light.

See the light

Light is made up of different colors, but light cannot be seen unless it hits our eyes. Light travels in straight lines, but it can change direction. When light passes through a prism (usually a three-dimensional glass triangle), it bounces off the sides of the prism and bends. Some colors in light bend more than others, so they spread out and you can see the different colors.

What is light?

Light is a type of energy called electromagnetic radiation, or EMR. "Electromagnetic" means it's made up of electrical and magnetic energy, and "radiation" means it spreads out from a source. Atoms—the tiny particles that make up everything around us— are that source. Atoms that have too much energy can get rid of it in the form of light.

The speed of light

Light travels in waves, a bit like waves that travel through water. Light travels faster than anything else in the universe— an amazing 186,000 miles per second (300,000 km per second)! It takes just eight minutes for light from the Sun to reach Earth.

Light doesn't always behave like a wave. Sometimes it behaves like it's made up of particles, so it spreads out more like a spray of water from a hose than waves in the sea.

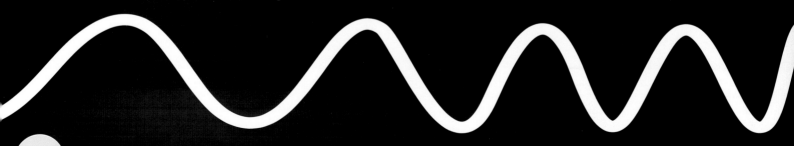

What is refraction?

Secrets of sound

When something vibrates, it squeezes and stretches the air around it, sending out waves that we hear as sound.

Echolocation

Some animals use sound to find their way around. This is called echolocation. Bats send out high-pitched squeaks that bounce off their surroundings. If their echo comes back quickly, it means there's something nearby.

Cymbals make large waves, which means a loud sound!

The speed of sound

Sound travels more slowly than light, at 1,125 ft per second (343 meters per second) in air. But the speed changes, depending on what the waves are traveling through. They can move four times faster in water than in air.

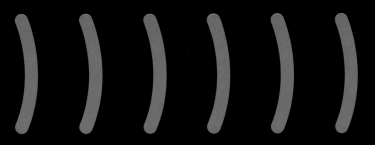

Curiosity quiz

Look through the "Light and sound" pages and see if you can identify the picture clues below.

Become an expert...

on visible light, pages 76–77

on how ears hear, pages 90–91

Refraction is when light waves bend, such as in a prism.

Now you see it...

Light waves (or electromagnetic waves) are all different lengths, but each length travels at the same speed. Some light waves are too short or too long for us to see. The light we can see is called "visible spectrum" light.

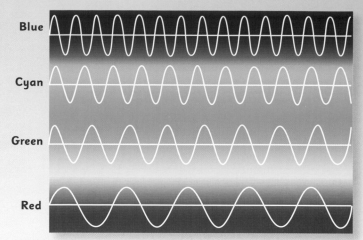

... And now you don't

Our eyes can see only light waves of a certain size—if they're longer or shorter, they're invisible. We use invisible electromagnetic waves in our lives every day.

Light of many colors

Visible light is made up of waves of different lengths. Each length appears as a separate color. For example, red waves are long and blue rays are short. Light contains an endless amount of colors. The only limit is on how well your eye and brain can tell one wavelength from another.

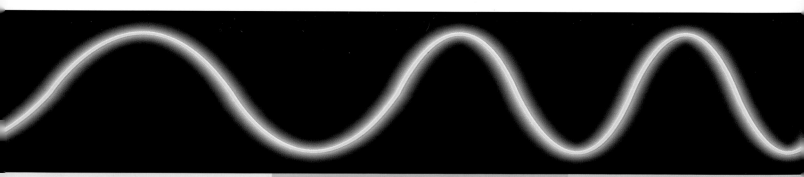

Radio waves	Microwaves	Infrared waves

Radio waves carry sound and images through the air. Radios, televisions, and cell phones all use radio waves. The longest radio waves can be 100,000 times longer than the shortest ones.

Microwaves heat water molecules in food and liquid, but they pass straight through glass and plastic. So when you heat soup in a microwave oven, it's not the microwaves that make the bowl hot, it's the hot soup inside.

Infrared waves carry heat. We can see infrared waves with night-vision goggles or special cameras, both of which are designed to pick up heat rather than light. When you get near something hot, it's infrared rays you feel on your skin.

What is white light?

Visible spectrum

Prisms and rainbows

Light bends when it passes through a prism. Each color bends at a different angle, so they separate out and form a rainbow.

A well-cut diamond is the best prism there is. Because it has so many different surfaces, light bounces around inside, creating bright, sparkly colors.

I can see a rainbow

When it's raining or misty, the tiny droplets of water in the air act like hundreds of prisms, breaking down sunlight into its different wavelengths. Each drop of water, depending on where it is, bounces a particular color into your eyes. You see these colors as the bands in a rainbow.

Visible	Ultraviolet (UV) rays	X-rays	Gamma rays

Everything we see can be seen because visible light waves bounce off objects. Light waves can come from the Sun and from light bulbs.

Ultraviolet waves come straight from the Sun. Some UV waves can burn your skin and, over time, cause wrinkles and cancer. That's why it's wise to cover up when you go outside in summer and put sunscreen on your skin to block out harmful rays.

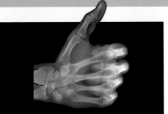

X-ray waves pass through most things, but not bones, teeth, or metal. When doctors want to look at your bones, they take X-ray pictures to see if anything is out of place or broken.

Gamma rays can bore through solid objects and kill living cells. Doctors use them in radiation treatments to destroy cancer cells. Gamma rays are also released when nuclear bombs explode.

All the colors of visible light appearing together.

Light and bubbles

When light hits the surface of a bubble, it reflects off both the outside AND the inside of its skin, producing the effect of swirling, shimmering colors.

Bubble colors

There are different colors in a bubble (purple, yellow, and blue) from those in a rainbow (green, blue, and red). This is because a rainbow splits white light into separate colors, but a bubble subtracts colors from light. If red is subtracted, you see the greeny-blue that is left behind.

These bubbles are on the surface of a soap and water solution.

Color secrets

You can tell how thick a bubble is by the colors it reflects. The blue parts of bubbles are thickest and the black parts are thinnest. Bubbles start to turn black when they are about to burst.

Hands On

Make your own bubble solution by mixing half a cup of dishwashing liquid with four cups of water and four tablespoons of glycerine.

What happens when you blow soap bubbles in cold weather?

Tiny planets

The patterns on a bubble look a little like the patterns of clouds around a planet. Both are thin films of fluid, so they act in a similar way. This is why some scientists use bubbles as model planets—they study the surface patterns to discover how storms and hurricanes develop.

The colors on the surface of a soap bubble appear to swirl around like a storm on a planet.

A storm has been raging on the planet Jupiter for 300 years.

Bubble shapes

The water molecules in bubble solution hold tightly onto each other, constantly pulling together. This means that bubbles always take up the smallest surface area possible.

When soap solution is stretched across a bubble wand, the smallest surface it can form is a flat plane.

When the solution is stretched around a pocket of air, the smallest surface it can make is a ball.

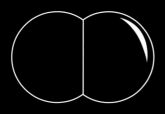

If two bubbles meet in midair, they shrink their surface area by forming a shared, flat wall between them.

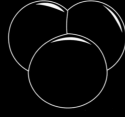

When three bubbles meet, they share three walls. The point at which these walls meet always measures 120 degrees.

Bursting bubbles

Soap bubbles burst when they touch anything that's dry (like a finger), or when the water in them evaporates.

Mirror, Mirror

When you want to see yourself, you look in a mirror. Mirrors reflect up to 95 percent of the light that hits them, while ordinary glass reflects only eight percent. How is this possible?

Working layers

When light hits a mirror, it bounces straight back in the direction it came from. You see an exact reflection in modern mirrors because they're made from glass that has several layers of metal and chemicals applied to the back. These give the mirror strength and stability, and make sure it offers a clear reflection.

Reflective silver layer (atoms shown magnified)

Backing

Glass

Fairground mirrors are deliberately bumpy (with concave and convex surfaces) to make people's faces and bodies look odd.

Convex mirror

Concave

Convex

Taking a curve

Curved mirrors give weird reflections and make you look very fat or thin. *Concave* mirrors dip in—they make things look larger but you see a smaller area reflected. *Convex* mirrors bulge out—they make things look smaller, but you see more.

Magnified silver crystals

Silver service

One of the best materials for creating reflections is silver. The crystals that form it have flat faces, so each one acts like a tiny mirror when light hits it. Polished silver, like many other metals, reflects light well and gives a sharp image. On its own, though, silver tarnishes in air, so to make mirrors, it's applied directly to glass, then other layers are added on the back.

When was the silvered-glass mirror invented?

Ancient images

Thousands of years ago, the only way people could see themselves was by looking into still water. In the middle ages, mirrors were made from polished stone, silver, bronze, or copper. These were very dark and the metals tarnished (got dull and discoloured), so they produced unclear images.

The world of mirrors

Even when you can't see them, there are mirrors everywhere!

Light-enhancing mirrors hung in wealthy homes for thousands of years. Before electricity was invented, they reflected candlelight.

Magnifying mirrors have a small, concave surface. They're designed to help in applying makeup or examining facial skin.

Dental mirrors help the dentist see all the hidden places inside your mouth. They're small, with a handle.

Rear-view mirrors are often convex to show a larger area. They're attached to bicycles, cars, and trucks so drivers can see behind them.

Car headlights and flashlights both have mirrors behind their bulbs to make their beams stronger and straighter.

Sunglasses sometimes have one-way mirror lenses. These are slightly see-through, so you can see the world, but other people just see mirrors.

Reflector telescopes have mirrors set inside them to help gather and focus light.

weird or what?

We all go through life without ever really seeing our own face—we can only ever see a reflection of it.

Mirror

Light

Mirror

Hide and seek

Periscopes use mirrors to bend light so that people can see around corners. A simple periscope is a tube with angled mirrors set parallel to each other at each end.

Spectators use mini periscopes to watch a golf tournament.

Military uses

Complex periscopes in submarines allow the crew to see the ocean's surface when they're underneath it. Periscopes are also used in tanks and gun turrets.

It was invented in 1835, in Germany, by a chemist named Justus von Leibig.

Lenses

Lenses are used to bend light to form an image. You have a lens in each eye, while telescopes and microscopes uses lenses to help us see things that are either too far away or too small to be visible.

What is a lens?

A lens is a transparent object that allows light to pass through it. Lenses can be curved on one or both sides. Lenses that curve inward are called concave. Lenses that curve outward are called convex.

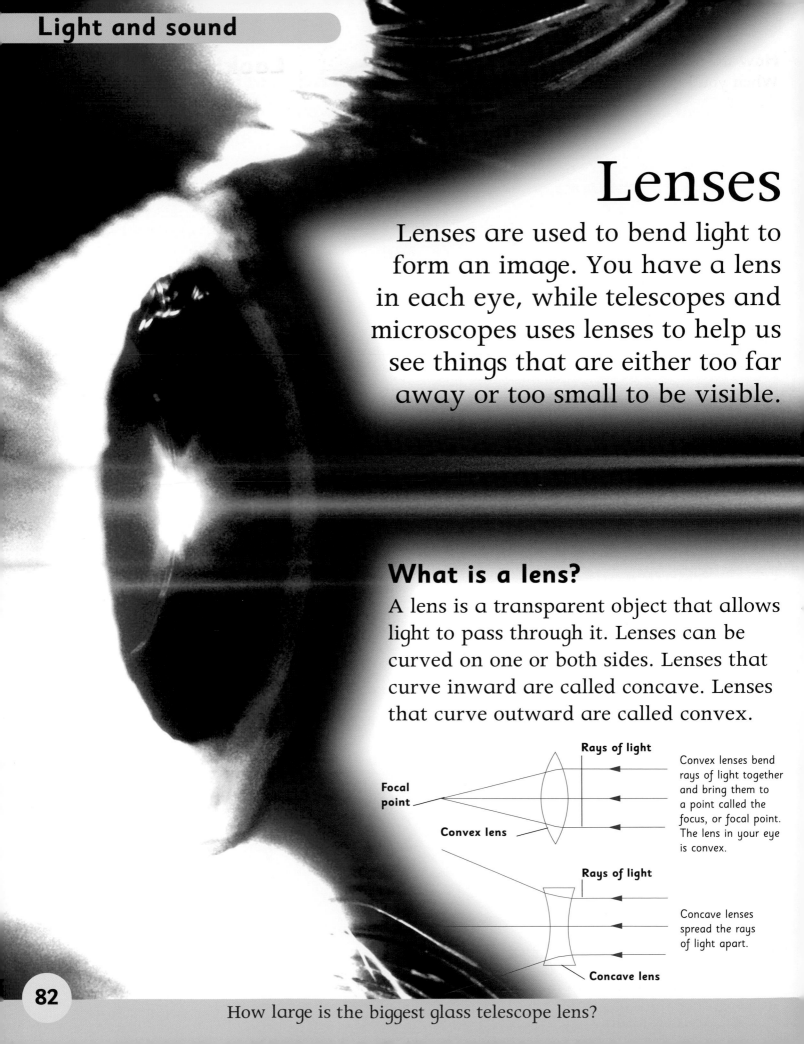

Rays of light

Focal point

Convex lens

Convex lenses bend rays of light together and bring them to a point called the focus, or focal point. The lens in your eye is convex.

Rays of light

Concave lenses spread the rays of light apart.

Concave lens

How large is the biggest glass telescope lens?

How do your eyes work?

When you look at an object, the light from it travels in straight lines to the lens of your eye. The lens focuses the light upside down onto the retina at the back of your eye. Cells in the retina turn the image into an electrical message. This travels to your brain, which turns the picture the right way up.

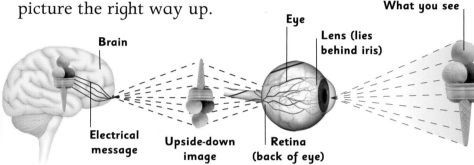

Brain

Electrical message

Upside-down image

Eye

Lens (lies behind iris)

Retina (back of eye)

What you see

That's better!

If someone is near-sighted, distant objects look blurred. This is because the lens focuses light in front of the retina instead of on it. If far-sighted, nearby objects are blurred, and light focuses behind the retina. Glasses or contact lenses help the eye focus light in the right place.

Near-sightedness

Before

Light focuses in front of retina.

Lens

Near-sighted people can focus on things up close but not in the distance. Concave lenses lengthen the light's path through the eye.

After

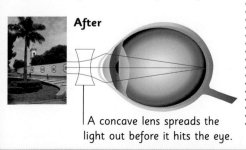

A concave lens spreads the light out before it hits the eye.

Far-sightedness

Before

Light focuses behind the retina.

Far-sighted people can focus on things in the distance but not on close objects. Convex lenses help shorten the light's path.

After

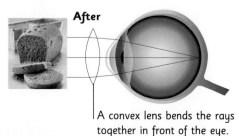

A convex lens bends the rays together in front of the eye.

Looking for lenses

You'll find lenses in all kinds of objects:

 Magnifying glasses are simple convex lenses that make things look bigger.

 Telescopes contain lenses that allow us to see things that are very far away.

 Microscopes make things that are too small for our eyes to see look bigger.

 Video projectors magnify images so they can be displayed on a screen.

 Some cameras have a number of lenses to produce different effects.

Bright light

Pupil shrinks in bright light.

Iris

Muscles around iris contract.

Dim light

Pupil expands in dim light.

Muscles around iris relax.

Instant reaction

There are muscles in the eye that help the lens change shape so you can change focus quickly to look at things that are near or far away. Other muscles around the iris control how much light enters the eye. Your pupils get bigger to allow more light in and help you see in dim conditions.

How light works

For thousands of years, the only light we had was from oil lamps, candles, and gas lamps. Then electricity was invented and we had lights we could switch on and off!

This is an X-ray of an energy-efficient bulb.

Basic bulbs

Traditional light bulbs contain a small coil, or filament, made from tungsten, a strong metal that can get incredibly hot without melting. When an electric current passes though the tungsten coil it gets so hot that it glows, and it's this glow that provides us with light.

Energy-saving light bulbs don't have a filament. Instead, they use electrodes to release tiny particles called electrons. These energize the gases inside the tube and make them glow. The light produced inside these bulbs is actually invisible, but a special coating on the bulb turns it into visible light. These lights are much cooler than traditional bulbs, last longer, and use less energy.

Wires inside the fixture carry electricity to electrodes.

Transformer boosts electricity to increase brightness.

Tungsten electrodes release electrons from electric current.

Glass tube contains argon and mercury gases.

LED bulb

LEDs can be used for signs and outdoor display screens. They give off a very bright light and come in lots of different colors.

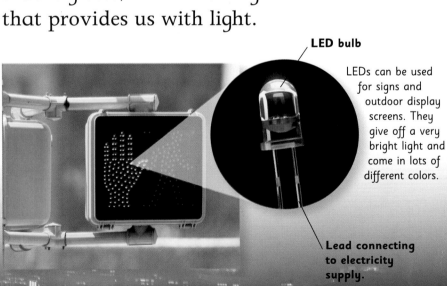

Lead connecting to electricity supply.

Small and bright

Very tiny light bulbs called LEDs (light-emitting diodes) are used in all kinds of electronic equipment, such as stereos, computers, and Christmas lights. They produce light by passing electricity through a special material that gives off light of one particular color.

How many bulbs are used to light the Empire State Building in New York City?

Mixing colors

Visible light looks white to us, but if you direct it through a prism it splits into different colors. You can reverse this process to turn different colored light back into white light. When you mix red, green, and blue you get white. Mix any two and you get magenta pink, yellow, or cyan blue.

Cyan Magenta

White light is a mixture of all colors.

Lasers

Lasers are devices that emit thin, powerful light beams. The light waves in a laser are all the same wavelength and line up exactly. This makes laser beams so intense they can cut through metal. Lasers are used in surgery, CD players, surveying, and industry.

Lasers are used to treat eye problems such as near-sightedness.

Laser surgery

Lasers are used for many types of surgery. The heat of the light is used to burn through tissue without cutting it with a scalpel. Lasers are also used to shatter kidney stones, and shape cavities for fillings in dentistry.

Lasers can be used in light shows and displays.

There are 3,194,547 bulbs.

Fireworks

Bursts of color and noise fill the sky—fireworks are packets of chemicals that explode when lit. A fuse ensures the explosion is delayed.

3, 2, 1, liftoff!

Light the fuse and stand back! The flame travels up into the firework, where it quickly sets fire to gunpowder inside.

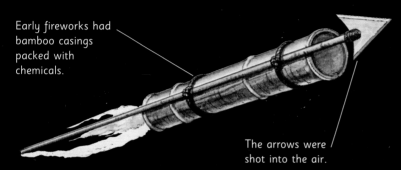

Early fireworks had bamboo casings packed with chemicals.

The arrows were shot into the air.

First fireworks

It's thought that the first fireworks were used in China more than 2,000 years ago. They were made from bamboo and used in religious ceremonies and to celebrate New Year.

Hi-tech displays

Firework displays are often run by computers. The computer sends an electric spark down a wire to light each fuse. It makes fireworks launch in the right order and explode at their highest points in the sky.

6. Explosion!
The chemicals inside the firework explode, releasing their energy as light, heat, and sound. Bang!

5. Stars
The gunpowder is mixed with stars—chemical mixtures that make a firework's flashes of color.

4. Gunpowder
Explosive gunpowder is stored in a chamber inside the firework.

3. Propellant
Inside the cardboard case, gunpowder burns quickly to shoot the rocket skyward.

2. Fuse
Fuse paper contains chemicals that burn steadily, allowing time for a person to stand back after lighting.

1. Launch tube
In big displays, fireworks are put inside metal tubes. These stay on the ground.

What is the firework called the Catherine Wheel named after?

Rainbow of color

Fireworks contain metallic salts—these make fireworks explode in different colors.

 Purple is made from Sr Cu stronium salts and copper.

 Red comes from Li lithium salts.

 Orange flashes are created by Ca calcium salts.

 Yellow color comes from sodium Na compounds.

 Green lights are made using barium Ba compounds.

 Blue flashes come from copper Cu compounds.

Firework patterns

When fireworks explode, they create different patterns in the sky. Here are six to look out for next time you go to a firework display.

Ring shell—a bright, expanding ring of stars.

Palm trees—stars move up as a "trunk," then spread out as "branches."

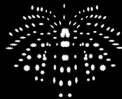

Crysanthemum—a pattern that leaves long trails of stars.

Serpentine—many stars that zigzag outward as they fall.

Fish—a swarm of stars moving randomly across the sky.

Willow—in this, star trails fall nearly all the way to the ground.

Measuring sound

All the sounds we hear are made up of waves that travel through the air to our ears. We can record the waves to see their shapes. Different sounds make different-shaped waves.

What is sound?

Sound is made up of waves of vibrations moving through the air. Any object that vibrates (moves quickly back and forth) can make a sound, just like this drum.

Hitting with a drum stick makes the drum skin **vibrate.**

A drum is a source of sound.

The skin of a drum is stretched very tight.

When you hit a drum its skin vibrates up and down. Sometimes you can even see the skin moving. As the skin vibrates, it pushes and pulls on the air around it, making the air vibrate, too.

Sound waves

Sound waves spread out in all directions from where they are made. As a wave moves through the air, the air molecules are squeezed together and then stretched apart.

Sound waves

Hands On

Hold one end of an rubber band on the edge of a table. Stretch out the other end and then pluck the band. Can you see vibrations and hear the sound they make?

Can you hear sound in outer space?

We can pick up sound with a microphone. Inside is a thin metal plate that vibrates when a sound wave hits it. The microphone turns the pattern of the vibrations into an electrical signal.

Microphone

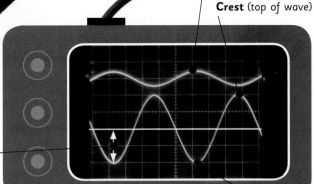

Flatter sound waves have a small amplitude. They sound quiet.

Crest (top of wave)

Taller waves have a large amplitude. They are loud sounds.

Oscilloscope

Trough (bottom of wave)

What sound looks like

Sound waves can be shown on a machine called an oscilloscope. The height of a wave is called its amplitude. The crests show where air is squeezed and the troughs show where air is stretched.

A loud, explosive storm

Slower than light

Sound waves travel more slowly than light. You can tell this during a thunderstorm. First you see the lightning, then you hear the thunder, perhaps several seconds later. Yet they happen at the same time.

Decibel levels

Loudness is measured in units called decibels. Here are some examples.

Leaves rustling
30 dB

Quiet music
50 dB

Speaking
60 dB

Vacuum cleaner
70 dB

Busy traffic
80 dB

Baby crying
85 dB

Pneumatic drill
125 dB

Jet engine
140 dB

! 85 dB

Listening to sounds of 85 dB and above for a long time can damage your ears.

Frequency and pitch

Frequency is the number of crests on a sound wave that pass by each second. High-frequency sounds, such as bird song, sound high-pitched. Sounds with low frequency, like thunder, are low-pitched.

Sonic boom!

Sound waves travel through air at about 750 mph (1,200 km/h). When a plane travels faster than the speed of sound, it creates sonic boom—a "shock wave" that makes a very loud noise.

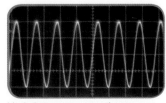

High-frequency sound waves

No. There's no sound because there's no air for sound waves to travel through.

How ears hear

Sound travels in waves. When these waves reach your ears, they're carried to your brain, which tells you what sound you're hearing—your mom's voice, for example, or the pop of a bursting balloon.

Ear, ear, ear

Your ears have three parts—the outer ear is the part you see. Your eardrum, which separates the outer ear from the middle ear, picks up sound vibration and passes it onto the three tiny bones of the middle ear. The inner ear contains bone, liquid, and tiny hairs.

Outer ear

The outer ear contains the ear canal.

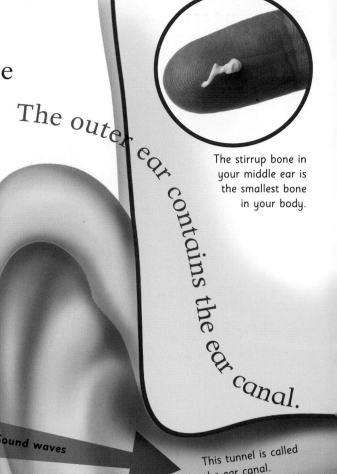

The stirrup bone in your middle ear is the smallest bone in your body.

Sound waves

This tunnel is called the ear canal.

The part of your ears that's on the outside of your head helps to "catch" sound waves. The strange folds in your ears help you work out when sounds are behind or above you.

Headphones let you hear one sound while blocking out others.

weird or what?

People often suffer hearing loss (deafness) when they get old. But if you listen to very loud music all the time, or sit too near the speakers at rock concerts, your hearing could be damaged forever.

Better than one

Ears are really very smart—they don't just identify sounds, they can also tell how far away they are, and which direction they're coming from.

The fact that sounds reach one ear before the other helps your brain to work out where they are.

Are there any sounds we can't hear?

All change

When sound enters your ears, it vibrates inside. The vibration is picked up by liquid in the inner ear, which vibrates slightly, causing tiny hairs to move. Cells at the base of these hairs transform the vibration into electrical impulses that travel along nerve pathways to your brain.

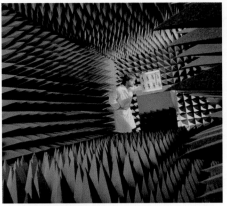

In an echo-free chamber, all the surfaces are lined with fiberglass wedges that absorb sound.

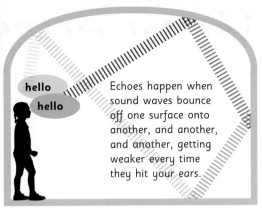

hello
hello

Echoes happen when sound waves bounce off one surface onto another, and another, and another, getting weaker every time they hit your ears.

Repeating sound

Sometimes you hear a sound once, then over and over again, getting fainter every time. This is called an echo. You can hear echoes in small spaces with hard walls, like wells, or where there are lots of hard surfaces all around—in a canyon, cave, or mountain range.

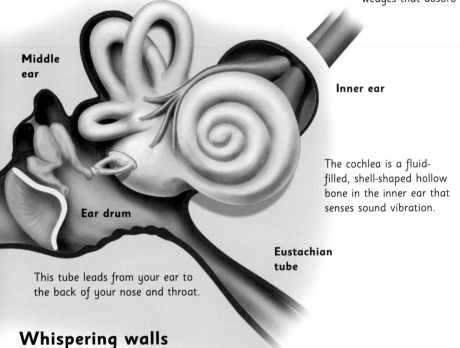

Middle ear

Inner ear

The cochlea is a fluid-filled, shell-shaped hollow bone in the inner ear that senses sound vibration.

Ear drum

Eustachian tube

This tube leads from your ear to the back of your nose and throat.

Helping ear

Hearing can get damaged or worn out. If any sound gets through, a hearing aid will make it louder. Cochlear implants do even more—they stimulate nerves in the cochlea, so they can help those who are totally deaf.

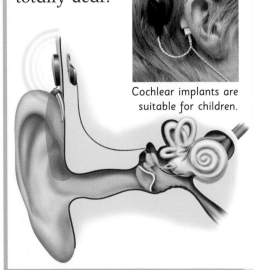

Cochlear implants are suitable for children.

Whispering walls

Sometimes, a hard, curved, surface causes sound to behave in strange ways. Visitors to the dam at the Barossa Reservoir in South Australia can whisper at one end, and someone at the other end—over 460 ft (140 m) away—can hear them clearly. This is because the curve causes the sound waves to bounce in a series of jumps that run all along the length of the wall.

Yes, dogs, snakes, and bats can all hear higher-frequency sounds than humans can.

Electric guitar

When you pluck the strings of a traditional (acoustic) guitar, the sound is magnified in the guitar's hollow body. An electric guitar's body is solid, but it still makes a very LOUD NOISE!

Pick

You can pluck the strings with your fingers or a **pick**.

Frets show the musician where to place her fingers to change the note.

Six or twelve metal **strings** are each tuned to a different note.

1 Pluck the strings

Play an electric guitar when it's turned off. The strings vibrate, but the sound they make is as quiet as a whisper.

The **neck** carries the fingerboard and supports the strings.

The **pickup** detects the vibrations of the strings.

The **solid body** is made from a single piece of wood.

The **bridge** has a **saddle** that lifts the strings clear of the pickups so they can vibrate easily.

An **amplifier** boosts the electrical signals to make the sound loud.

3 Amplified

The electrical signal travels from the pickup along a wire to the amplifier. The amplifier strengthens the signal, and a built-in loudspeaker blasts out the sound.

2 What picks up the sound?

When you turn on the guitar, the pickups start working. Pickups are made of wire wrapped around a magnet. The magnet has a magnetic field around it. When strings vibrate they change the pattern of the magnetic field, sending currents through the coil to the amplifier.

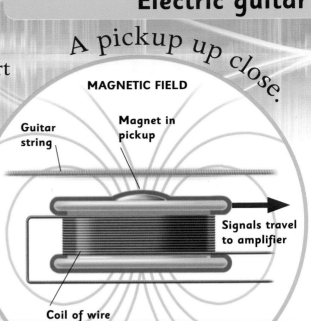

A pickup up close

MAGNETIC FIELD

Guitar string

Magnet in pickup

Signals travel to amplifier

Coil of wire

MAGNETIC FIELD

Machine heads are like screws and can be twisted to tighten or loosen the string for tuning.

Volume and tone control knobs

Pickups convert vibrations from the strings into electrical signals.

Electric current The electrical signal from the pickups travels through wires to the controls, then onward to the amplifier.

Coil of wire in pickup

weird or what?

The electric guitar was first championed by jazz musicians. They loved the way this loud instrument let them be heard above the noise of a brass band.

Different electric guitars

Guitars come in all sorts of shapes and sizes. The shape of an electric guitar does not affect its sound.

Semi-acoustic guitars are a mix of electric and acoustic, with hollow bodies.

Double-headed guitars let musicians switch sounds without switching guitars.

Bass guitars only have four strings and play the lower notes in a piece of music.

Custom guitars are whatever shape or size a musician prefers.

Bits and bytes

Digital technology relies on the silicon chip and the binary code. Data that is sent to and from digital appliances is sent in binary digits called bits. It is measured and stored in bytes.

Silicon chips and computers

Personal computers were made possible by using silicon to make microchips. Silicon was chosen since it's a good semiconductor—it can keep the flow of electricity going or make it stop.

Bit
A **bit** is a binary digit and can be either a 0 or a 1. Each bit can hold the answer to one simple question, using 0 for "No" and 1 for "Yes."

Byte
A **byte** is made up of 8 bits and is the measurement unit used to describe the storage capacity and transfer rate of digital systems.

1 **kilobyte** is 1,024 bytes
1 **megabyte** is 1,024 kilobytes
1 **gigabyte** is 1,024 megabytes
1 **terabyte** is 1,024 gigabytes
1 **petabyte** is 1,024 terabytes
1 **exabyte** is 1,024 petabytes

8237635UA8
MALAY
X 247

Sand covers over half the Earth's surface.

Ever heard of silicon?
Silicon and oxygen make sand—and there is a LOT of sand in the world!

Lump of silicon

Shallow mantle

Lower mantle

Outer core (molten)

Inner core (solid)

Crust and lithosphere

How many transistors can fit on a single silicon chip?

What's inside?

A silicon chip contains millions of transistors (things that control the flow of an electric current) and other tiny electronic parts that are all connected to each other.

A silicon chip can be very small—less than $1/10$ square in (1 cm^2) and about $1/10$ inch ($1/2$ a mm) thick.

Silicon wafer

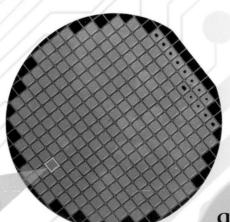

Pattern to be etched on chip.

How is a silicon chip made?

Electronic circuit patterns are photographed onto disks of silicon, called wafers. Chemicals are used to etch the patterns into the silicon in several layers. The wiring that connects up the circuit is made in the same way.

Individual chips

Wafers are tested to make sure they work. After being checked they are cut into individual chips, which are placed into protective cases.

Individual chip from wafer

Finished chip in package.

Hundreds of chips can be made on a single wafer.

Curiosity quiz

Look through the "Bits and bytes" pages and see if you can identify the picture clues below.

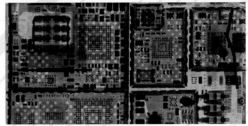

Become an expert... on binary code, pages **98–99** on the Internet, pages **110–111**

Some silicon chips contain two billion transistors.

Inside a laptop

We use computers to do all kinds of things—play games, watch videos, and surf the Internet. All these things are controlled by a microprocessor that acts like a tiny electronic brain.

Laptop computer

All the components of a personal computer can be built into a convenient folding package the size of a book. Some laptops use wireless technology to interact with printers, scanners, and other devices by radio waves.

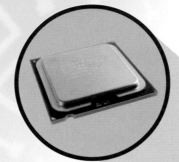

The microprocessor, or central processing unit (CPU), is the single most important chip in a computer. This electronic circuit is what makes all the programs run. It is hidden inside the computer.

The hard drive is where all the computer's programs and data are stored permanently. Most laptops can store up to 100 gigabytes of data.

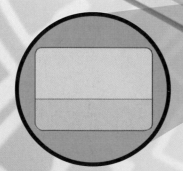

Instead of a mouse, a trackpad is used to control the cursor on screen. By dragging a finger over the trackpad and clicking buttons it is easy to scroll vertically and horizontally, or open and close windows.

DVDs or CDs can be played or copied on this drive.

Address Book
Business
Calculator
Calendar
Dictionary
ASPN

What is a netbook?

English

Area

Japanese

Results

Sign post

Quick search

12

Picture search

INDU

AAPL

1d 1w 1m 3m 6m 1y 2y

Laptop and computer screens use hundreds of tiny red, green, and blue liquid crystal cells to produce an image, just like a television.

Computer talk

 Memory holds data that the CPU needs to read and write quickly.

 Hard drive saves files and programs when the computer is switched off.

 Mobile broadband dongle connects laptops to the Internet wirelessly.

1MB **Bytes**—all data on a computer is held in units called bytes.

 Cables connect the laptop to input devices, printers, and the Internet.

 Input devices include computer mice, joysticks, and drawing tablets.

Ports provide connections to external devices. An MP3 player, digital camera, or external hard drive can be plugged into various ports. You can also transfer your photos and videos using a memory card slot.

A light sensor activates the illuminated keyboard in low-light conditions.

97

It's a small, lightweight laptop designed for Internet access on the move.

Binary code

The binary code is made up of two digits: one and zero. The code converts images, text, and sounds into numbers in order to send information from one digital device, such as a computer, to another.

Binary numbering
Computers use binary numbers because they are easier to handle. In binary, the digits (read from the right) are worth 1, 2, 4, 8, and so on—not units, tens, and hundreds. In ordinary numbers, "1,001" is one unit, no tens, no hundreds, and one thousand. But in binary "1001" is one 1, no 2, no 4, and one 8, which equals 9.

How a motherboard works

The motherboard is the main circuit board in a computer. It connects all the main parts and passes on instructions.

2. I/O controller make the central processing unit (CPU) pause.

1. Keyboard communicates with motherboard via input/output (I/O) controller.

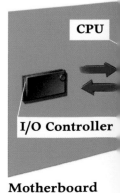

CPU

I/O Controller

Motherboard

How many ones and zeros can a fiber-optic cable carry per second?

Hands on

Using the code below you can write out your name in binary code. Use uppercase letters for the beginning letter of your first and last name and lowercase for the remaining letters.

Sending numbers

Fiber-optic cables are used to transport binary numbers from one computer to another. An electric current carries the numbers as a stream of digital data. A laser turns the current into pulses of light that are sent through the fiber-optic cable.

ASCII Code: character to binary code

0	0011 0000	F	0100 0110	U	0100 0101
1	0011 0001	G	0100 0111	V	0100 0110
2	0011 0010	H	0100 1000	W	0100 0111
3	0011 0011	I	0100 1001	X	0100 1000
4	0011 0100	J	0100 1010	Y	0100 1001
5	0011 0101	K	0100 1011	Z	0100 1010
6	0011 0110	L	0100 1100		
7	0011 0111	M	0100 1101		
8	0011 1000	N	0100 1110		
9	0011 1001	O	0100 1111		
A	0100 0001	P	0100 0000		
B	0100 0010	Q	0100 0001		
C	0100 0011	R	0100 0010		
D	0100 0100	S	0100 0011		
E	0100 0101	T	0100 0100		

For lowercase letters replace the first four digits with 0110. The rest of the code is the same as uppercase, so a = 0110 0001.

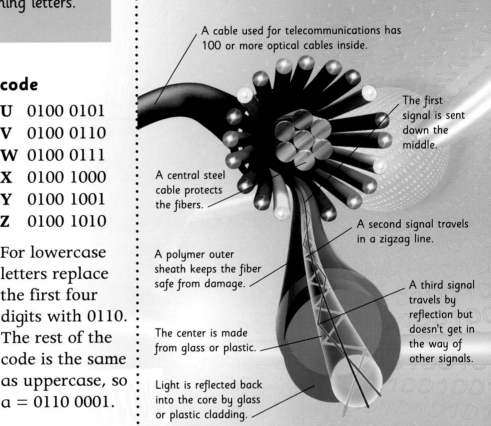

A cable used for telecommunications has 100 or more optical cables inside.

The first signal is sent down the middle.

A central steel cable protects the fibers.

A second signal travels in a zigzag line.

A polymer outer sheath keeps the fiber safe from damage.

A third signal travels by reflection but doesn't get in the way of other signals.

The center is made from glass or plastic.

Light is reflected back into the core by glass or plastic cladding.

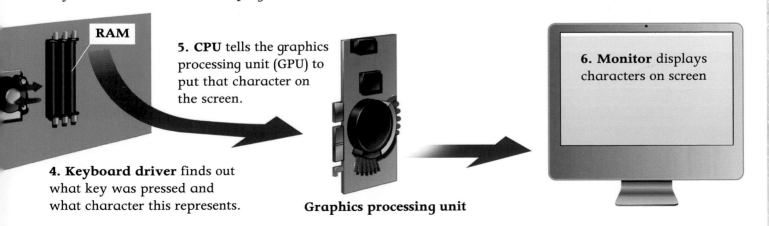

3. Central processing unit (CPU) stops what it is doing and accesses memory (RAM) to run the keyboard driver built into the program.

RAM

5. CPU tells the graphics processing unit (GPU) to put that character on the screen.

6. Monitor displays characters on screen

4. Keyboard driver finds out what key was pressed and what character this represents.

Graphics processing unit

100 billion ones and zeros per second at almost the speed of light.

Bits and bytes

Sharing data

When you send an email or a message on your cell phone, how does it know where to go? In fact, it is passed around a huge series of computers that are connected to each other by wires or radio.

Without a wire

Wireless systems, such as Bluetooth, allow two or more electronic gadgets to transmit data without plugging them into each other. Wireless technology is very effective over short distances, but it cannot transmit very far.

weird or what?

Bluetooth is named after King Harald Blåtand I of Denmark. He united Danish tribes into one kingdom. The inventors felt that was what Bluetooth does—it unites different devices into one system.

How far?

Bluetooth can connect up to eight gadgets at the same time as long as they are within about 30 ft (10 m) of each other. Bluetooth can operate over greater distances if a more powerful transmitter is used.

Radio wave

Using Bluetooth, you can transfer music, speech, and videos between gadgets, as well as send instructions. There is a Bluetooth-operated robot, for example.

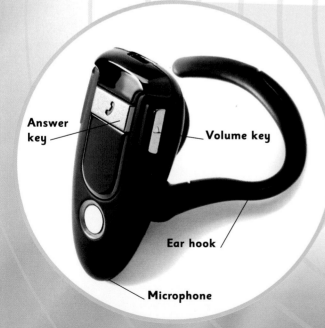

Answer key

Volume key

Ear hook

Microphone

A Bluetooth headset allows wearers to answer their phones without actually holding it. That's useful if you are carrying things or driving a car.

How does it work?

Just like TVs and FM radios, a wireless system uses radio waves. It chops up data into manageable pieces and transmits that data in separate chunks as radio waves. The receiving device, such as a phone or computer, picks up the radio signals and puts the data back together.

100

What is the world's fastest home Internet connection speed?

What are computer networks?

Towns and cities are joined together by a network of roads. Computers are also linked together by networks. The scale of a network can be as small as a home computer and printer or as big as hundreds of computers used in an office.

Most homes connect to the internet through a telephone or cable-TV socket. From there, data can be sent to other rooms by a hub.

Telephone or cable socket

Telephone exchange

The majority of computer networks connect with each other using telephone lines. When you send an email it may have to travel along hundreds of miles of telephone wires and through several networks to reach its destination.

What are hubs and routers?

A hub sends information to every device connected to it. They are mainly used in homes and small networks. Routers allow large numbers of computers to communicate and direct data between networks.

What is a server?

Computer networks rely on servers to access and store information. There are different types of server. Businesses often use a file server to back up documents every day so that work isn't lost. FTP (File Transfer Protocol) servers are used for sending and receiving files. Mail servers are used to store millions of emails for company networks.

Networks

There are many different types of network used to link computers:

PAN — **Personal Area Network** Used for single-user devices.

LAN — **Local Area Network** Joins small groups of computers, like an office.

CAN — **Campus Area Network** Links university campus LANs into one network.

MAN — **Metropolitan Area Network** Connects all the networks in a city.

WAN — **Wide Area Network** A network that covers a large area, like the Internet.

GAN — **Global Area Network** A future network of wireless computer networks.

Antenna

Wireless routers send and receive data through their antennae. The router then directs the data to exactly the right computer. Hubs have to try every device on the network to get the right one.

40 gigabits per second—it can download a DVD in 2 seconds!

Early cell phones weighed about 1½ lb (800 g).

Today's phones weigh as little as 1½ oz (40 g).

Early phones

In the 1980s phones were as big as a brick, about six times the size of phones today.

Cell phones

Spread out across the world is a network of tall metal towers, called base stations. When you make a call from your cell, the call travels to the nearest base station, which sends it on an incredibly fast journey to the phone of your friend. It only takes seconds to connect to your friend's phone.

In addition to making phone calls, the iPhone can act as an iPod music player with a fast Internet connection.

Base station

In the countryside, base stations cover larger areas than in cities. This is because there are fewer people living in rural areas, so fewer people use the network.

Mobile cells

Cell phones work within a network of cells. Each cell is covered by a base station. You can only make a call if you are close enough to a base station.

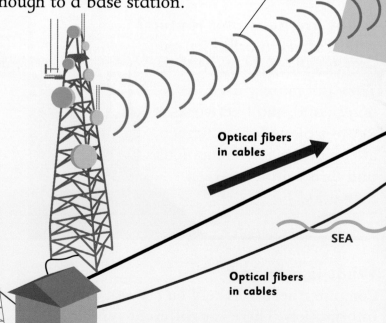

Microwave link

Optical fibers in cables

SEA

Optical fibers in cables

Cell phone

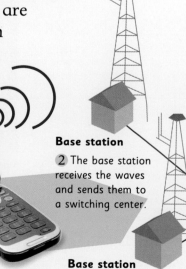

1 A cell phone converts sound into radio waves. It sends out these waves to the nearest base station.

Base station

2 The base station receives the waves and sends them to a switching center.

Switching center

Base station

3 The switching center sends the waves to another switching center, either as microwaves or through optical fibers in cables under the ground or sea.

What does SIM stand for?

What does it do?

Cell phones have lots of good features and some bad ones.

 Make calls, send texts, make video clips, and take photos.

 Play music, download video clips, and watch television programs.

 Find directions, get train schedules, and download listings of what's going on.

 Phones create waste, since they can take hundreds of years to break down.

weird or what?

Every minute all over the world 1,000 people buy a cell phone for the first time. There are more than three billion cell phones in the world and more are made each day.

Cell phones use lithium-ion batteries that give roughly seven hours of talk time.

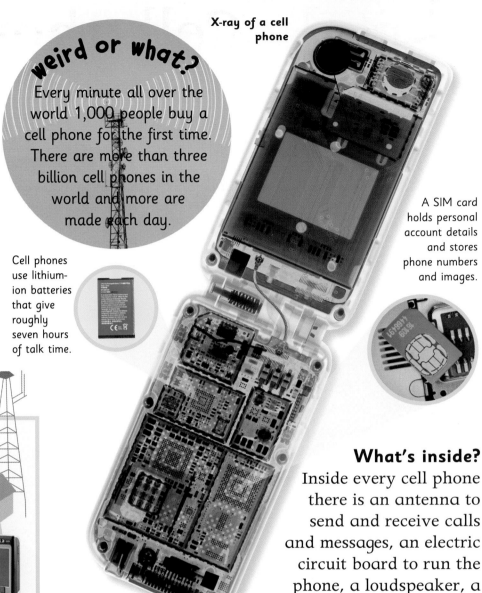

X-ray of a cell phone

A SIM card holds personal account details and stores phone numbers and images.

What's inside?

Inside every cell phone there is an antenna to send and receive calls and messages, an electric circuit board to run the phone, a loudspeaker, a microphone, and a battery to provide power.

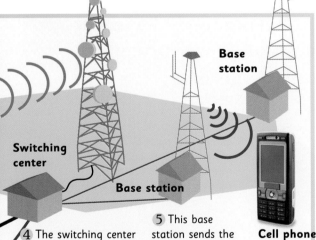

Base station

Switching center

Base station

Cell phone

4 The switching center sends the waves to another base station.

5 This base station sends the waves to another phone.

Text messages travel in the same way as sound waves. Billions of text messages are sent every day.

Future phones

New types of phone are developed all the time. These watch phones will be available soon. Phone handsets may not even be used in the future if scientists make phones small enough to put in your head or your ear.

Watch phones

It will be hard to lose a watch phone if you're wearing it!

Digital photography

Digital cameras allow you to capture a moment in time, such as blowing out your birthday candles. They are also used in space exploration and medical science.

Lens   **Shutter**   **Viewfinder**

Flash
When it is too dark to take a photo, a built-in flash briefly lights up the scene.

Canon DIGITAL IXUS 95 IS
CANON ZOOM LENS 3x IS 1:2.8-4.9 6.2-18.6mm
10.0 MEGA PIXELS

Snap away!

Digital cameras vary in size, from a small camera on a cell phone to a large professional studio camera. People usually own a compact camera like this one.

From light to a digital file

So how does a camera actually take a photo? It's a simple process that requires the following in order to work: light, a shutter, a lens, a sensor, and a memory card.

Light is made up of three primary colors: red, green, and blue. These colors make up all other colors. All three combined make white light.

The sensor is a grid of millions of pixels.

1 Light is reflected off a scene. The camera's shutter opens, so this light can pass through the lens to a sensor inside the camera.

2 The sensor is covered in tiny squares, called pixels. Each pixel measures the amount of red, green, or blue light that hit it. They turn this into electrical signals.

3 The signals travel to the camera's memory system, where they are stored on the memory card.

How many pixels are in a megapixel?

View, focus, take!

Some digital cameras have a viewfinder to allow photographers to see what they want to photograph. Other cameras just have a screen on the back of the camera for composing a shot.

Seeing an image

Images shown on a digital camera screen are made up of thousands of tiny pixels. When you look at all the pixels together they make a complete image.

Battery

Most digital cameras use rechargeable batteries.

Memory card

Images are stored on removable memory cards until you download them onto your computer.

The dial allows the user to choose different settings such as the flash or close-up shots.

The most exciting thing about taking digital photos is viewing them! You can download images by inserting a memory card into a computer or through a cable attaching a camera to a computer.

Editing and playing with photos

Digital photos can be edited and changed in special computer programs. You can play with an image, make it black-and-white, or you can fix red-eye. Try out the examples below.

Convert to black-and-white

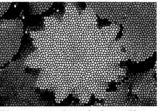

Play around with fun effects

Fix red-eye

Happy birthday!

Add text to an image

Saving memories

Old-fashioned film cameras store images directly onto plastic film, whereas digital cameras record photos on a memory card. Memory cards are measured in megabytes (MB) and gigabytes (GB) and vary in size, from a small 512 MB to a large 32 GB! They are likely to get bigger in the future.

Bits and bytes

Who invented radio?
Guglielmo Marconi is credited with building the first radio system. In 1901, he transmitted radio signals across the Atlantic Ocean.

Radio and TV

It's hard to imagine life without radio or TV. We use both for information and entertainment. There are millions of programs, but how do they get to our radios and TVs?

How do radios work?

First called a wireless, the radio didn't need wires to connect the transmitter and receiver.

Speech and music are turned into electrical signals by a microphone in a **radio studio**.

The **electrical signals** from the speech and music travel through wires to a **radio transmitter**.

The **radio transmitter** sends out radio waves from the radio station.

Traditional radio sets pick up the radio waves and turn them back into speech and music.

Digital transmission
Digital radios also use a transmitter, but the waves they use are different from those of a traditional radio.

What's inside?
The main parts of a radio are an antenna, a circuit board with a tuner and amplifier, and a loudspeaker.

Digital radio
When you listen to a digital radio there is little or no interference, such as hissing noises. Digital transmitters send out sound codes all mixed up together so that interference can't affect them much and your radio will usually be able to understand them.

Digital radios use codes made from lots of ones and zeros. They are transmitted over a large band of radio waves.

Tucked behind the radio is the antenna. This picks up radio waves.

Inside the radio is a tuner and a computer chip that decodes the waves and converts them into sound.

What does LCD stand for?

A neon lamp sent light into holes in a spinning disk.

First TV

The scientific research for televisions began in the late 1800s. Baird's televisor was the first ever TV to work. A rotating disk transformed light from a scene into lines forming a moving image.

Baird's televisor

Images on the televisor were grainy. The mechanical system was soon replaced with a better quality electronic system.

The light coming through the spinning disk lit up a scene and made a moving image. The red light from the neon lamp made the image appear red.

TV inventor
John Logie Baird demonstrated the first television broadcasts in 1929.

Transmission today

Television stations transmit programs through electrical waves.

Television pictures are created by **cameras** in **TV studios**.

Programs are sent out from the TV studio **over wires** or **microwaves**.

Programs can be sent up to **satellites** in space and then sent back to Earth.

Satellite dishes can pick up the microwaves and send them to TVs along a cable.

A TV turns the waves into the pictures and sound that make up a TV program.

LCD TV

LCD screens have been used since the 1970s in calculators and watches, but only recently for TVs. A modern LCD TV screen is made up of millions of tiny squares called pixels.

If you look very closely at an LCD TV screen you can see the pixels.

Color squares
Pixels contain blue, red, and green. When the pixels are turned on or off the colors merge, forming pictures.

weird or what?

There are roughly 1.5 billion television sets in the world. That's one TV for every four people on the planet.

Liquid-crystal display.

Bar codes

Bar codes make shopping faster and more convenient. When a scanner reads an item's bar code—beep!—it sends a code to a computer. The computer sends back information about that item, including its price.

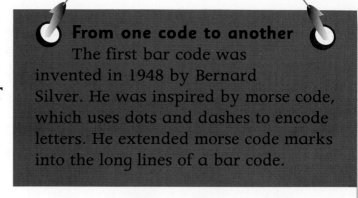

From one code to another
The first bar code was invented in 1948 by Bernard Silver. He was inspired by morse code, which uses dots and dashes to encode letters. He extended morse code marks into the long lines of a bar code.

S A L E

What is a bar code?
The black and white stripes of a bar code represent a string of numbers—a code that is unique to a single product. Various types of bar code exist. The type shown here is used throughout Europe.

Where's it from?
The first number in a bar code tells you the country where the product was made. Every country has its own number: 50 means the UK, and anything from 00 to 13 is in the US and Canada.

Who makes it?
This is the code number of the manufacturer who made the product. All products made by that manufacturer will all have the same four-digit code.

5 012345

Manufacturer's logo

When was the first bar code used?

What's your number?

Each number in a bar code is represented by two white stripes and two black stripes of different widths. The long, thin guide lines at the edges and center of the code tell the scanner to start reading.

Scanner

Right-hand guide

Center guide

5 012345 678917

Left-hand guide

Machine readable part
The scanners you normally find in the supermarket are known as "omni-directional" scanners. They emit laser light in a starburst pattern that can read the bar codes at any angle.

Human readable part
If the scanner is unable to read the bar code, the cashier can input the numbers.

Scanning the goods

The scanner shines a narrow beam of light onto a bar code. A light sensor inside the scanner measures the reflected light. White lines reflect more light than black lines, which is how it tells the difference.

What is it?
This is the code for the product itself. The code number for this item is 567891.

The check digit
This number is used by the scanner to check whether it has read the data correctly.

2-D bar codes

These new bar codes are scanned from top to bottom as well as left to right. Some of them can be read by cell phone cameras and webcams and take you straight to a website.

678917

Some 2-D bar codes, like this Quick Response code, can store hundreds of times more information than ordinary bar codes.

On June 26, 1974, for a pack of chewing gum.

The Internet

People first heard of the Internet in the early 90s, but it had special uses (mostly military and educational) before then. Now, about 1.5 billion people use it—a quarter of the world's population.

What is the Internet?

It's simply a network that links computers around the world. Try imagining it as a huge map (or spider's web), with all the strands linked by different pathways.

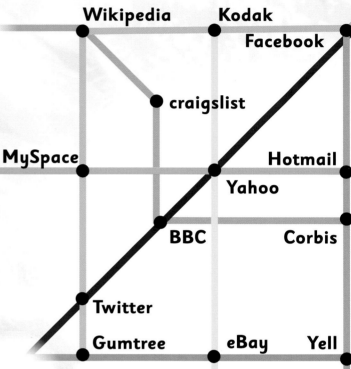

Wikipedia   Kodak
Facebook
craigslist
MySpace   Hotmail
Yahoo
BBC   Corbis
Twitter
Gumtree   eBay   Yell

WWW

The World Wide Web

Applications like the World Wide Web let you use the Internet for information, entertainment, and communication. People can even build their own website for other people to use, creating a "global village."

In 1998, there were 26 million unique web pages on the Internet. In 2008, experts estimated that there were over a trillion of these pages.

INFORMATION

Find out about almost any subject that catches your interest by entering a few key words in a search engine.

GAMING

People all over the world play each other at MMOGs—massively multiplayer online games.

SHOPPING

Buy anything from a vacation to a vacuum cleaner without stepping outside. Everyday, billions of things are sold online.

CHATROOMS

Make new friends in other countries and hold real-time conversations with them by logging on to a chatroom.

What's Wi-Fi?

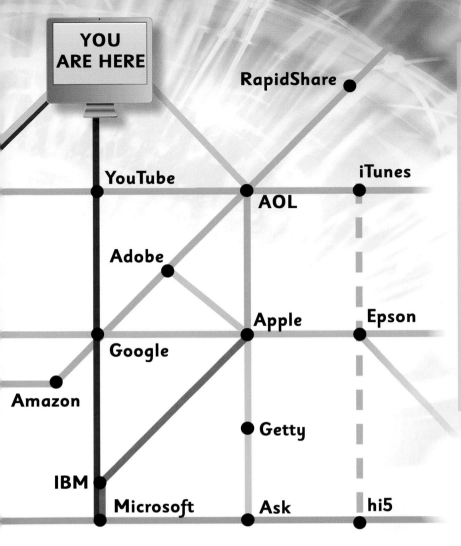

YOU ARE HERE

RapidShare

YouTube

iTunes

AOL

Adobe

Apple   Epson

Google

Amazon

Getty

IBM

Microsoft   Ask   hi5

Internet terminology

Surf—To look at web pages on the Internet and navigate through them.

Browser—Computer program that connects with a WWW server.

Router—Device for routing Internet traffic.

Search engine—Site that holds a database of website addresses.

ISP—Internet Service Providers link computers to the Internet.

URL—stands for Uniform Resource Locator—a complete web address.

HTML—HyperText Markup Language is the language in which web pages are written.

Chunks of data

Internet information is split into parcels or packets before it is sent. A packet carries a portion of the original text and the addresses of the computers it's traveling between.

Press send

The transfer of data on the Internet happens when the packets are sent to their destination. It's called packet switching.

Broken link

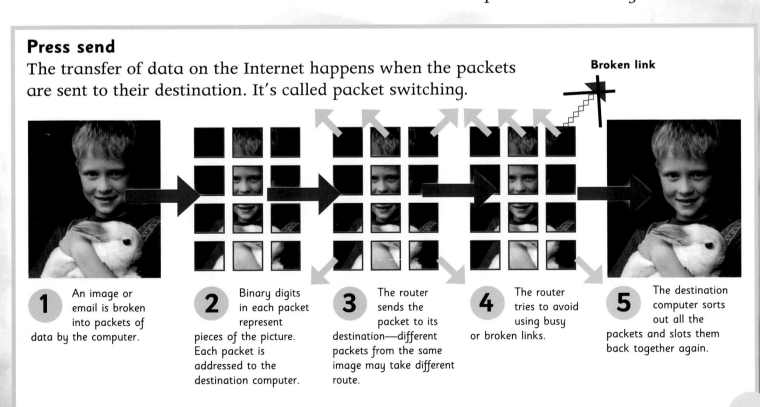

1 An image or email is broken into packets of data by the computer.

2 Binary digits in each packet represent pieces of the picture. Each packet is addressed to the destination computer.

3 The router sends the packet to its destination—different packets from the same image may take different route.

4 The router tries to avoid using busy or broken links.

5 The destination computer sorts out all the packets and slots them back together again.

It's the technology that lets you access the Internet using radio waves instead of cables.

Search engines

The Internet contains a vast amount of information, and finding what you're after can be tricky unless you know how to look. Search engines are a useful tool, since they do all the hard work for you.

How do search engines work?

Search engines use special robots called "spiders." These spiders search the Internet for new pages. They target websites that have a lot of traffic (people visiting them), then spread out to other web pages. The search engine lists the words on those pages and makes them into an index.

1 Web spiders search the internet for new web pages.

Apple	Highchair	Pianos
Backtrack	Iceland	Quail
Birch	Internal	Rested
Clearance	Jock	Sage
Dinner	Kilt	Sesame
Dinosaurs	Labrador	Souffle
Eating	Minimize	Traffic
Fruits	Orange	Uniform
Gluttonously	Organic	Unleaded
Hearing	Peony	Vest

2 Search engine lists the words on each page the spiders find.

Bundle
Binary
Bicycle
Biceps
Banana

3 Search engine keeps an index of all the words it finds.

4 A user types in a word.

bicycle

Good-quality bicycles
Children's bikes
Bicycle bargains
Bicycle

5 Search engine checks its index to find any relevant pages.

Bicycle bargains
Massive savings on bikes
www.bikesZ129.com

Children's bikes
New and used bicycles for children
www.NandUbikes3000.com

Good-quality bicycles
Buy brand new bicycles at cheap prices
www.cheapbikesforu99.com

6 Search engine lists these pages for the user in matter of seconds.

Where did the search engine Google get its name?

Web   **Images**   **Videos**   **Maps**   **News**   **Shopping**   **Mail**   **More**

Meta data

Websites often have key words (meta data) embedded in them. Businesses make sure their web pages contain these words in the title and subtitle of a web page. Web-page designers can also highlight certain words to make sure search engines pick them up.

Complex searches

If you type in an exact quote, a question, or a few key words, a search engine will look for these words within web pages. These are literal searches, so they look for your exact wording. You need to be clear, or you won't find the information you want.

Searches

airplanes

British airplanes

British airplanes, 1940s

British airplanes, 1940s, used in WW2

If a website has lots of visitors, it's more likely to come first in a list.

Top of the list

Companies try to make sure that their web page comes at the top of all the search-engine lists. They do this by putting key words on the site, or by paying search engines to put an ad for their company on the first page.

Search terms

Working with the Internet involves lots of special words and expressions.

Web browsers access the Internet. Firefox and Safari are web browsers.

http:// will appear in front of most Internet addresses you open.

http stands for Hypertext Transfer Protocol, an information-transfer system.

Bookmarks give you quick access to your favorite sites.

History facilities list recently accessed sites so you can go back to them.

Tags are key labels given to bookmarks or files so you can find them fast.

weird or what?

If a business doesn't want to be listed in searches, it can build a robot-exclusion protocol into its website so search spiders will ignore the page.

The word "googol," which stands for the number 1 with 100 zeros after it.

Robots

Robots are machines that work for us. Most robots work in factories, but some do jobs at home. Some look like machines, but others look like humans.

The robot vacuum cleaner is powered by rechargeable batteries.

Home help
A robot vacuum cleaner moves around a room on its own, sucking up dust. To find its way, the robot sends out sound waves. These bounce off walls, tables, and chairs so the robot knows where they are.

Cars are made by robots on a production line. The robots are controlled by computers and powered by motors. The computers turn the robots' motors on and off to make the robots move.

A robot arm has joints like your arm. Instead of a hand, it has a tool called an end effector. This means the robot can do work such as pick up metal panels or tighten screws. Effectors often have built-in pressure sensors so the robot knows how hard to hold things.

Robot workers
Industrial robots are connected to the ground. They have an arm with a tool on the end for doing jobs such as packing boxes or welding metal.

How smart is the most intelligent robot?

Swarm robotics

A new kind of robots, called swarm robots, work together on a task. Some swarm robots attach themselves to each other to make one machine. Others work like ants, completing projects as a team.

When ants work together, they can move a heavy apple.

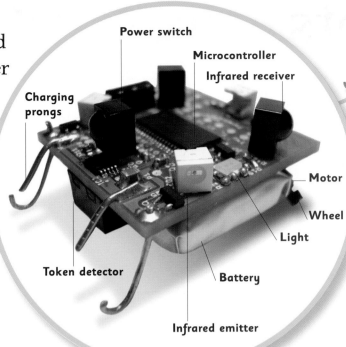

Formica—actual size

Formica robot

This mini robot uses infrared light to "talk" to other robots on its team. It can be programmed to perform different tasks, such as moving tokens toward a light.

Power switch
Microcontroller
Infrared receiver
Charging prongs
Motor
Wheel
Light
Token detector
Battery
Infrared emitter

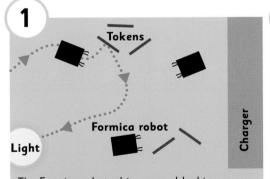

1

Tokens
Formica robot
Light
Charger

The Formica robots drive around looking for tokens to push toward the light.

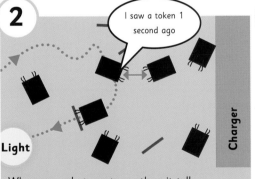

2

I saw a token 1 second ago

Light
Charger

When one robot meets another, it tells it how long ago it saw a token.

3

I saw a token 60 seconds ago

Abandon search; return to charger

Light
Charger

The robots haven't seen a token for a while, so they return to the charger.

Bomb squad

A remote-controlled robot can go to places that are too dangerous for humans. It has a steel claw that can carry away a bomb.

Kismet robot head

This robot reacts to its human carer like a baby. It can look happy, sad, or frightened. When it is left alone for too long, it looks lonely. When it is overwhelmed by lots of movement in front of it, it closes its eyes and sleeps.

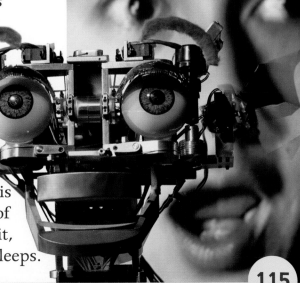

About as smart as an insect.

115

Near future?

The future seems like years away, but it is actually just around the corner. Some fantastical gadgets are already in prototype stage and could be in our lives very soon.

The house of the future

The house of the future will be watching you. It will wake you up, run you a bath, and even prepare breakfast without being asked. Even the chores will be done for you.

Xanadu Homes

The Xanadu House was designed and built in Florida. It was the pioneer for future houses, with hi-tech energy-saving designs and automated rooms.

Computers will sense radio tags in clothes and objects to keep track of everything.

Computerized rooms

The rooms of the future will be fully automated. Computers will monitor your daily routines, so the house computer can adapt and keep the house fully stocked, energy efficient, and neat.

weird or what?
The fridge of the future could also do your shopping. It will keep track of what food you are eating and will order more online. All you'll have to do is get hungry and eat.

Computers will turn lights on and make sure your favorite TV show is recorded.

Roof and walls are made from a special plastic foam.

The plastic (polyurethane) foam traps heat and lowers energy bills. It is also quick and easy to build with.

When was the first Xanadu House built?

Life recorder

Every year computer chips get smaller and store more information. Imagine a wearable gadget, such as a necklace, that can store everything that happens in your life. The Momenta neck-worn PC would work like an airplane's black-box, which records every moment of a flight. Photo albums will be a thing of the past, as your happy moments are recorded and stored.

Sensors touching the skin could detect pulse and medical data, so the necklace could call for help in a medical emergency.

The camera is activated by an increase in your heart rate. So all your exciting and funny moments are captured.

A large memory allows long recording times, so you don't miss anything.

Communication pole

The Xanadu House used computers to run it—from an auto-chef in the kitchen to a talking security computer.

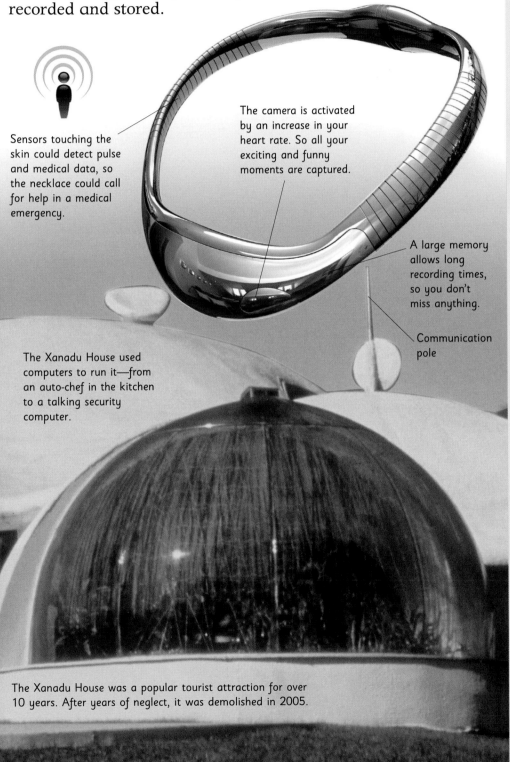

The Xanadu House was a popular tourist attraction for over 10 years. After years of neglect, it was demolished in 2005.

Future foods

Foods of the future could be modified to give the human body the right balance of nutrients. Genetically modified (GM) crops could also hold the key to help farmers around the world to grow in poor soil conditions, so nations suffering from drought could grow enough food to survive and prosper.

GM technology is very expensive and there are concerns that crops could be harmful.

Eye contact

The contact lens of the future will do more than improve your vision. It will have tiny projectors that will beam information directly into your eye. So, 3-D movies, navigation aids, and in-eye data will be available at the blink of an eye.

The thin lenses will use solar power so they are always charged.

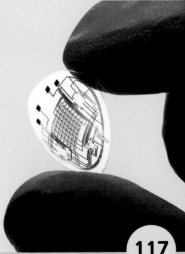

The first experimental Xanadu House was built in Wisconsin in 1979.

In the future

Commuter shoes

Powered shoes will allow people to travel faster than walking. Just pull the wheels down and tiny, powerful, electric motors will take you to work.

Wireless sensors in the shoes communicate with each other so they work together, keeping you going in the right direction.

The Embrio concept

This motorized unicycle will be able to transport two riders. Sensors, gyroscopes, and computer assistance keep it balanced, and it uses clean fuel cell technology.

Riders sit in the saddle like a modern-day motorcycle.

Acceleration is controlled on the handlebar.

Riders have to lean from side to side to steer.

Stabilizers engage at low speeds.

The hydrogen bus

Soon, polluting buses will be a thing of the past. DaimlerChrysler has developed a bus that runs on liquid hydrogen and oxygen. The only by-product released into the atmosphere is water vapor.

The BitCar

The scientists at the Massachusetts Institute of Technology (MIT) are developing the BitCar. It will use satellites and cameras to help you navigate, and is stackable to save space. It will also use clean fuel cell technology.

Pick up a BitCar from the side of the road then drive and drop it off at your destination.

How far is the Moon from the Earth?

Space vacations

In the near future space will become the ultimate luxury vacation destination. Soon, space planes will fly to the edge of space, and for a couple of minutes, give vacationers amazing views of the Earth, as well as a taste of floating in zero-g.

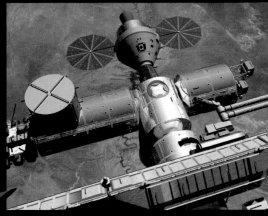

Destination Moon By 2020, scientists are planning to revisit the Moon with a new craft called Orion. Humans last set foot on its surface in 1972. In the near future, there could be a spaceport and even hotels on the Moon.

Virgin Galactic will soon be offering suborbital flights that give a taste of space.

The International Space Station

The International Space Station (ISS) is the only place in space where humans can live. In the near future, space hotels could be orbiting Earth.

The ISS orbits Earth every 90 minutes and can be seen by 90 percent of the world's population.

The first part of the ISS was launched in 1998. By 2010, the finished station will be the size of a football field.

Space vacation
So far there has only been one space tourist. Dennis Tito paid millions of dollars to spend a week on board the ISS.

At the moment there are only three working Space Shuttles. They are going to be retired in 2010.

Dennis Tito

119

Not-so-near future

The distant future offers many fantastic possibilities. Scientists could upgrade our brains, invent computer doctors who can heal at the touch of a button, and discover how to copy the way the Sun works.

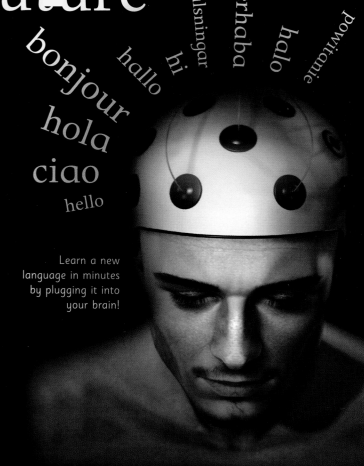

bonjour
hola
ciao
hello
hallo
hi
hälsningar
merhaba
halo
powitanie

Learn a new language in minutes by plugging it into your brain!

Brain upgrade

To upgrade a computer, new computer chips, memory boards, and software are plugged in and loaded. The brain of the future could be upgraded in a similar way. The first plug-in modules could offer better memory, reactions, or language skills. Even entertainment could be tuned in, with 3-D shows and even smell-o-vision.

When the rain falls and temperature drops, clothes will become watertight and thick.

Clothes may even change color to match other clothes and accessories.

Smart clothes

No more taking sweaters off in the future. Smart clothes could change their properties in response to changes in the weather. A shirt could allow air through when it's hot, but become watertight in rain, and even bulletproof in an emergency! Clothes will be woven from smart, adaptive molecules that are controlled by electric or magnetic fields.

When did the first Zeppelin airship take to the skies?

Fusion power

One day we'll run out of oil, gas, and coal and need another way to make power. The answer is in the stars. Stars make a lot of energy, so if we could make our own mini-star on Earth we could make almost unlimited energy. That's exactly what a fusion reactor does. There are experimental reactors around today, but no one's managed to get them to make much power yet. But where does star fuel come from? It's just hydrogen, which is all around us in water.

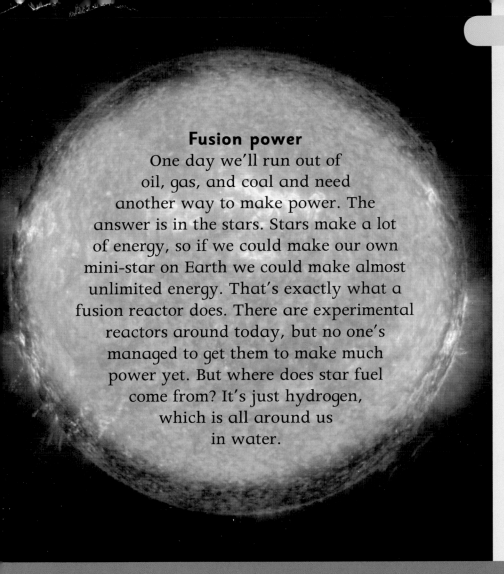

Auto-Doc

This sounds like something from a TV show, but in the future the Auto-Doc machine could keep you in good health.

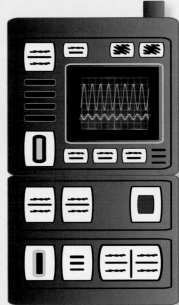

Sensors will analyze your breath and blood, or scan your body.

After diagnosis, the Auto-Doc may be able to prescribe drugs or make pills.

Return of the airship

Popular in the first half of the 20th century, airships could be seen in our future skies. Powered by clean solar energy and helped by the wind, these giants of the sky won't need to refuel. Although they will be slower than a plane, they will be able to lift heavy loads, making them perfect for cargo flights, or they may be luxury hotels in the clouds.

Without needing to refuel, the airship of the future could take you around the world in one nonstop trip.

The first Zeppelin airship flew in 1900.

Glossary

accelerate To go faster. When a moving object's velocity (speed) increases, it is accelerating.

aerodynamics The study of the way gases move (especially air), and the way things move in air (such as airplanes).

amplifier Something that increases the power of an electrical signal without changing its shape.

amplitude The height of a wave, such as a sound wave, from its peak (top) to its trough (bottom). The bigger the amplitude, the more energy a wave has. A sound wave with a large amplitude is loud.

atom The smallest particle of a particular element.

biofuel Fuel made by or from living things. Wood, alcohol made from corn, and biogas made from garbage are all biofuels.

binary code A code made up of the digits 1 and 0. Digital technology (computers) converts all letters and numbers into binary. For example, the letter A can be coded as 01000001.

bit The smallest unit of memory used by a computer. The word "bit" is short for "binary digit."

buoyancy How well an object can float in a liquid or a gas.

byte A group of eight bits.

carbon emissions Gases containing carbon that are released into the air, especially when fuel is burned. They may cause global warming.

circuit A loop that an electric current travels around.

concave When an object curves inward, like a bowl, it is concave.

conductor A material that lets electricity or heat pass through. Metals are conductors.

convex When an object curves outward, like the back of a spoon, it is convex.

coolant A liquid or gas that cools things down.

current The flow of electricity from one place to another.

data Another word for "information," especially digital information.

decibel A unit that can be used to describe how loud sound is.

density The weight of a solid, liquid, or gas in relation to its size. A dense material has lots of atoms packed closely together. Less dense objects float in more dense fluids. Wood can float in water because it is less dense than water.

digital Describes a machine that works by using numbers. Digital watches display the time in numbers rather than on a dial. Digital technology, such as computers, stores data in binary code.

displacement The amount of fluid (a liquid or gas) that is moved by an object placed in the fluid. An egg dropped into a glass of water will displace some water. The amount of water displaced has the same volume as the egg.

What is g-force?

download To copy files from the Internet to your computer.

drag A force that slows an object down as it moves through air or water. The faster the object moves, the more drag there is.

efficiency How much of a machine's energy is turned into useful work. An energy-efficient light bulb turns more of its energy into light than a normal one.

electromagnet A magnet created by a flow of electricity through a coil.

electron A tiny particle inside an atom. It carries a negative electrical charge.

element A chemical element is a substance that cannot be broken down into any other substances. The atoms in an element are all of one kind—they all have the same number of protons.

energy The ability to do things (such as walk or move an object). Something that can supply energy is called a power source.

fiber-optic cables Flexible tube containing thin, bendable glass fibers that carry information in the form of light waves.

fluid A liquid or a gas. The atoms in a fluid can move freely to fill space.

force A push or a pull. Gravity is the force that keeps you on the ground.

fossil fuels Fuels that come from the earth and are the remains of living things. Coal, oil, and gas are all fossil fuels. They are not renewable sources of energy.

friction A force that makes things slow down. When two solids rub against each other, or when a solid moves through liquid or gas, it causes friction.

fulcrum The point, or pivot, that a lever turns on.

gearwheel A wheel with "teeth" around the outside that can connect to and turn another gearwheel. A toothed wheel that connects to a chain is called a sprocket.

geothermal power Power that comes from natural heat within the earth.

gravity A force that pulls objects toward each other. The pull of Earth on an object is called its weight.

horsepower A unit used to measure a machine's power. It was first used to describe how powerful a steam engine was compared to a horse.

hydraulic A hydraulic machine has pipes filled with fluid. Hydraulics help increase forces such as lifting, pulling, or pushing so a machine can work more efficiently.

hydroelectric power Electricity that is made using the power of water, such as using a flowing stream to turn a turbine.

The force of gravity on an object.

Reference section

inertia The resistance of an object to a change in movement. An object that is stationary (not moving) will try to stay still, and an object that is already moving will try to keep moving in a straight line and not change direction.

insulator A material that does not let electricity or heat pass through it easily. Wood and plastic are insulators.

internal combustion engine An engine that burns fuel inside the engine to create power.

kinetic energy The energy an object has when it moves. The faster it moves, the more kinetic energy it has.

LCD This stands for "liquid crystal display." LCD screens display pictures or numbers by applying an electric voltage to liquids that act like crystals.

lens An object that bends light rays to make an image.

lever A simple machine made up of a bar moving on a fulcrum. Using a lever magnifies or reduces a force to make a job easier. Seesaws, wheelbarrows, and tweezers are all levers.

magnetic field The area around a magnet where other magnets are attracted or repelled.

magnify To make bigger.

mass How much substance an object has.

metadata Information (such as key words) in a computer file that describes the content. For example, a file of a picture might have metadata that tells you how big it is or when the picture was taken.

molecule Two or more atoms joined together. A water molecule is made up of three atoms—two hydrogen atoms and one oxygen atom.

momentum When an object is moving it has momentum. The heavier the object is and the faster it moves, the more momentum it has. The more momentum it has, the harder it is to stop it from moving.

motherboard The main circuit board of a computer or other large electronic gadget.

nanotechnology Technology that can build things from atoms and molecules—the very smallest parts of an object or material.

neutron Inside an atom's nucleus are neutrons and protons. Neutrons have no electrical charge.

nuclear energy Power that comes from the energy released by the atoms of certain elements.

nucleus An atom is made up of a nucleus and electrons. The nucleus is made up of neutrons and protons.

orbit The path an object in space takes around another. For example, the Earth orbits the Sun.

patent An official record of an invention that registers who made it so no one else can claim they did.

photovoltaic panels Panels that collect solar energy (sunlight) and turn it into electricity.

pixel A small colored square that makes up part of a picture on a computer or TV screen.

potential energy The energy stored in an object that is raised above the ground. It changes into kinetic energy when the object falls.

prism A triangular glass block used to split light into visible colors.

What are turbines?

proton Inside an atom's nucleus are neutrons and protons. Protons have a positive electrical charge.

pulley A wheel that has a rope around it used to move a load.

reflection When light waves bounce off a surface (such as a mirror) and change direction, they are reflected.

refraction When light waves travel through a transparent object (such as a window or glass prism), the light bends. This is refraction.

renewable energy Power that comes from the Sun, wind, water, or geothermal sources. Unlike fossil fuels, it will never run out.

resistance A force that pushes against movement and slows down a moving object. In electricity, resistance measures the voltage needed to give a particular current.

satellite A natural or man-made object that moves around a planet. The Moon is Earth's natural satellite. Man-made satellites circle the Earth and send back information on things like weather.

solar power Power that comes directly from the Sun.

solution One substance dissolved in another.

streamlined A streamlined object has smooth curves so that air or water flows over it with as little resistance as possible.

technology The science of how things work.

thermostat A device that controls temperature, for example, on a heating system or a boiler.

thrust A force that moves something forward. Engines provide thrust for planes and cars.

transistor A part in an electric circuit that controls the flow of electricity.

velocity Speed in a particular direction.

voltage The force that makes electrons move in an electric current.

wave An up-and-down or back-and-forth movement that carries energy from one place to another.

weight The pull of gravity on an object gives the object weight. It is not the same as mass. On Earth, an object has mass and weight. In outer space, where there is no gravity, the object's mass stays the same, but it has no weight.

zero-g Zero gravity is a feeling of weightlessness. If something has no gravity pulling it toward the ground, it floats freely, like an astronaut in outer space.

Machines with blades that turn when gas (such as air) or liquid flows past them.

Index

Picture credits

The publisher would like to thank the following for their kind permission to reproduce their photographs:
(Key: a-above; b-below/bottom; c-center; f-far; l-left; r-right; t-top)

Courtesy of Motorcycle-USA.com: 37br; **Alamy Images:** 19th era 6cra; A Room with Views 7tl; Judith Aronson / Peter Arnold, Inc. 80tr; Roger Bamber 80-81ca; Stephen Bond 6tr; Mark Boulton 73cra (recycling point); Mike Brand 91bl; Scott Camazine 56bl; Chesh 92bl; Tony Cordoza 83cra (projector); David Noton Photography 15cr (crane), 18-19; Danita Delimont 8br; GabiGarcia 34b; GS International / Greenshoots Communications 73crb; Horizon International Images Limited 74-75 (sun and yellow sky); D. Hurst 7fbr, 49fbr, 102cra, 123t; Leslie Garland Picture Library 19tr, 95crb (radio circuit), 106cra; Oleksiy Maksymenko 96ca, 103ca (phone battery), 103cla (BlackBerry); Mindset Photography 87cr; Motoring Picture Library 24tl; National Mot or Museum / Motoring Picture Library 61cra (central locking); David Pearson 21tr; Mark Phillips 73bl; PVstock.com 85tr; Helene Rogers 96clb; Rolf Hicker Photography 9br; Ian Shaw 11br; Adrian Sherratt 8cra (fire welding); Stockfolio 532 87br; Studioshots 105fclb; The Print Collector 26bl; Hugh Threlfall 96-97c; Joe Tree 106br (digital radio); Colin Underhill 43cra (aircraft), 50-51 (main image), 126tc; Wolfgang Usbeck / Bon Appétit 68bc (chicken in oven), 68crb; View Stock 86clb; Tony Watson 37cb, 127b; WidStock 65tr; Jochem Wijnands / Picture Contact 58br; WildLife GmbH 79cr; WoodyStock 101cla; Jerome Yeats 7cl; **Courtesy of Apple:** 96clb (trackpad), 96crb (hard drive); Photo: **Beiersdorf AG:** 13fbr (plaster); **Bombardier Recreational Products Inc. (BRP):** (®, TM and the BRP logo are trademarks of Bombardier Recreational Products Inc. or its affiliates, www.brp.com —BRP, a privately held company, is a world leader in the design, development, manufacturing, distribution and marketing of motorized recreational vehicles. Its portfolio of brands and products includes: Ski-Doo® and Lynx™ snowmobiles, Sea-Doo® watercraft and sport boats, Evinrude® and Johnson® outboard engines, direct injection technologies such as Evinrude E-TEC®, Can-Am™ all-terrain vehicles and roadsters, as well as Rotax® engines and karts) 118bl; **Bresslergroup:** Momenta PC 117ca, Momenta PC 117tl; **Courtesy of Canon (UK) Ltd:** 13tr, 95cr, 104cla, 104tr (insert), 105cla; **Corbis:** A2070 Rolf Haid / DPA 52br, 53bl (insert); Mike Agliolo 98ca (background), 98cl, 99cr (background); Arctic-Images 118cra; Jeffrey Arguedas / EPA 23cra (truck), 29 (main image), 128br; David Arky 84cra (light bulb), 92tr; Bettmann 5tr, 6cl, 52clb, 107cla (photo inserts); Richard Broadwell / Beateworks 1cl, 64cr (light bulb); Burke / Triolo Productions 9cra; Car Culture 25clb, 39tr; Ron Chapple 63crb (corn), 67br; Chogo / Xinhua Press 41crb (Qinghai-Tibet railway); Claudius 43crb, 57crb (turbines -close up), 64cl; Chris Collins 88br; Construction Photography 45br (brick), 63cra (hydroelectric power); Angela Coppola 120bl (boy); Jim Craigmyle 92c; Nigel J. Dennis / Gallo Images 89bl; Rick Doyle 32tr; Robert Essel NYC 81cra (rear-view mirror); Shannon Fagan 111b (boy with rabbit); Randy Faris / image100 64crb (recycling); Thomas Francisco 75cr, 81tl; Martin Gallagher 115fcra; Glowimages 87tr; Andrew Gompert / EPA 81br; Ole Graf 15cra (fulcrum), 16-17b (seasaw); Mike Grandmaison 63bl; Richard Gross 67tl; H et M / photocuisine 65br; Don Hammond 46-47 (main image); Philip Lee Harvey / Photoconcepts 120bl (grass); Dallas and John Heaton / Free Agents Limited 41cra (Bullet train); HO / Reuters 47tr; Hulton-Deutsch Collection 7cra (Sinclair C5), 7tc, 26cla, 26tl, 107tr; ImageShop 2cra; ION / amanaimages 93bl; The Irish Image Collection 65cla; Simon Jarratt 43br, 63cra (solar power), 67cra (solar power); Mark A. Johnson 63cr (tidal power); Jose Luis Pelaez, Inc. 77br; Karl-Josef Hildenbrand / DPA 113cra (search engine browser); Kulka / zefa 13cra (sheep); Patrick Lane / Somos Images 98l; Larry Lee Photography 65cra (insert); Larry Lee 48-49 (main image); Lester Lefkowitz 32ca; Leng / Leng 64cr (laundry); Ted Levine 32cla (diver); Barry Lewis 53cra, 65clb (flames); Yang Liu 57cr, 62tr; Gerd Ludwig 63cla; David Madison 25br; Sadao Maejima / AmanaImages 87tl; Lawrence Manning 6fbr, 27cra; MM Productions 64tr (gardening); Moodboard 12bl (light bulb), 23cb, 23cra (welder), 32cla (welder), 64cra (television); Roy Morsch 118cla; Noah K. Murray / Star Ledger 43cra, 52tr; Charles O'Rear 9bc (coins); David Papazian / Beateworks 64cra (insulation); Louie Psihoyos 95tc; Radius Images 62l; Nick Rains 41cra (Australian); Anthony Redpath 120fbl (rain); Jim Reed 89cl; Roger Ressmeyer 63crb (geothermal power), 67cb; Reuters 119bl; Michael Rosenfeld / DPA 2-3 (circuit board t & b); Schlegelmilch 35cl; Sie Productions 32fcla; Julian Smith 85cr; Paul A. Souders 57tl; Specialist Stock 47bc; Pauline St. Denis 64cra (walking); Hubert Stadler 25cra (waterwheel); George Steinmetz 1bl, 48crb (gas burning), 65bl, 115br; Keren Su 60crb; Ramin Talaie 119cla; Tetra Images 106fcla (microphone); Transtock 37cl; Bernd Vogel 103cla (man with phone); Karl Weatherly 75cra (rainbow), 77tl; Westend61 15cra (lake), 17tr; William Whitehurst 77cra; Bai Zhiyong / Xinhua Press 1br, 26-27c; **Dorling Kindersley:** Anglo-Australian Observatory, photography by David Malin 60bl (galaxy background); British Library 10cla; Design Museum, London 89cra (vacuum cleaner); Exeter Maritime Museum, National Maritime Museum, London 8fclb; © Firepower, The Royal Artillery Museum, Woolwich 24cb; Glasgow Museum 11ca, 107ca (early television); London Planetarium 10ca; Marconi Instruments Ltd 75crb (oscilloscope screen), 89bc, 89ca; Mark Hall Cycle Museum, Harlow Council 26clb; Jamie Marshall 12fbl, 57bl, 105crb; Judith Miller / Wallis and Wallis 61ca (handbag); National Motor Museum, Beaulieu 11bl (early car), 31bl; National Railway Museum, York 40cla; Stephen Oliver 57cra (unlike poles), 60cra; David Peart 48crb (diver); Pitt Rivers Museum, University of Oxford 8cl; Anthony Pozner, Hendon Way Motors 81cr; Guy Ryecart, courtesy of Renault 57cl; Science Museum, London 4bc (Faraday's induction ring), 4bl (refractometer), 4bl (telephone), 4br (electric), 4br (spectacles), 4fbr (Wimhurst voltage), 5bl (teamaker), 5br (microscope), 5fbl (camera), 5fbr (radio amplifier), 6bc, 6bl, 8cb, 8cla, 8clb, 9fcra (compass), 10br, 11cla (Edison's lamp), 11fcla, 94cl, 95cl; Toro Wheelhorse UK Ltd 30bc; Paul Wilkinson 12cla (car), 23ca, 28bl; York Museums Trust (Yorkshire Museum) 9clb; **Electrolux:** 114tr; **Electronics and Computer Science, University of Southampton:** Rob Spanton (formica.ecs.soton.ac.uk) 115t ("Formica" bot); **Ernestomeda s.p.a.:** Zaha Hadid / DuPont™ Corian® / Scholtès - "Z. Island by DuPont™ Corian®" 116cra; **Getty Images:** AFP 31br; Colin Anderson / Photographer's Choice 22l; artpartner-images / Photographer's Choice 96-97 (background); Rob Atkins / Photographer's Choice 15crb (crane close-up), 19tc; Benelux Press 95br, 114b (main image); Don Bishop / Photodisc 113cra (computer); Alex Cao / Photodisc 6-7; Car Culture 38b; Frank Chmura / Nordic Photos 43crb (power lines), 59br; Jeffrey Coolidge / Photodisc 97crb (memory stick); Tony Cordoza 107bl (TV); Crowther & Carter / Stone 110-111 (background); Davies and Starr / Stone 113crb (tags); Peter Dazeley / Photographer's Choice 83cla (ice cream); Mary Kate Denny / Photographer's Choice 87crb (green); Digital Vision / George Diebold 67bl; Digital Vision / John William Banagan 87crb (red); Jody Dole 7br (old mobile phones), 11crb; Michael Dunning / Photographer's Choice 77fbl; Laurence Dutton 103cra; Ben Edwards 81cra (dental mirror); Joshua Ets-Hokin / Photodisc 17tl; Don Farrall / Photodisc 6cla; Joe Fox / Photographer's Choice 76br; Gerard Fritz / Photographer's Choice 112-113 (background); Adam Gault / OJO Images 83cra (microscope); Dave Greenwood / Photonica 16cra (tweezers); Karl Grupe / Photonica 117cra; Darrell Gulin 105cla (camera screen), 105tc (pixel insert); Alexander Hafemann / iStock Exclusive 63cra (wind power); Bruce Hands 40cra; Tim Hawley / Photographer's Choice 113bl; Chris Hondros 4cra (camera film.); Lyn Hughes 43 (background), 45l (sky background); Hulton Archive 4tr, 10cb; Janicek 73cra (battery); Brian Kennedy / Flickr 40bl; Keystone / Stringer / Hulton Archive 52c; Bruce Laurance / The Image Bank 76bl; Romilly Lockyer / The Image Bank 42 (clouds background); Vincenzo Lombardo / Photographer's Choice 16cra (door handle); Steve McAlister 22cra, 113crb (document); Ian Mckinnell 4cra (pool ball); Ian Mckinnell / Photographer's Choice 13crb; Ryan McVay / Photodisc 25cra (steering wheel); Ryan McVay / Photodisc 6br; Ryan McVay / Stone 88bl; Jose Maria Mellado 20c; Steve Mercer / Photographer's Choice 113cra ('http'); Peter Miller 70-71 (snow flakes); Joos Mind / Stone 104bl; MJ Rivise Patent Collection 4cl; Bruno Muff / Photographer's Choice 97tr; NASA / Science Photo Library 79tc; Hans Neleman 34tr; Joseph Niepce / Hulton Archive 10cra; noa images / Digital Vision 113cr; Thomas Northcut / Digital Vision 75clb; Thomas Northcut / Photodisc 100bl, 101br, 101clb; Thomas Northcut / Stockbyte 84fclb; Jose Luis Pelaez 77bl; PhotoLink / Photodisc 61crb (lightning in insert); Pier / Stone 87crb (yellow); Pier / Stone 75crb (gray); PM Images 13cr (wheelchair); Steven Puetzer / Photodisc 84clb; Terje Rakke 41crb (brakes); RNHRD NHS Trust 13cr (x-ray); Lauri Rotko 15cl; Chad Slattery / Stone 53tc; Stocktrek Images 36tl, 119cb; Studio MPM / Stone 100crb; Paul Taylor 15br, 20cra; The Image Bank / Garry Gay 87crb (orange); Travelpix Ltd / Photographer's Choice 84-85b; **iStockphoto.com:** 13tr, 36cb (cyclist), 61cra (credit card), 81 (face in mirror), 102tl (modern mobile phone), 106cl (digital radio transmitter), 106l (digital radio transmitter & background), 107cr (transmission icons), 112ca; Kseniya Abramova 36-37b (horses); Arndt Design 41bl; Black Ink Designers 106br (sound waves); Sascha Burkard 76bc; Caziopeia 103clb (3/4 angle mobile); Kenneth Cheung 102ftl; CreativeChain Design House 104-105t (background); Luca di Filippo 102bl; Elton Dralle 28cr; Blaz Erzetic 1clb, 109tc; Jamie Farrant 90cb (speaker insert); Nadezda Firsova 100-101 (background); Robert Hadfield 81crb (sunglasses); Jaap Hart 84-85t (ray background); Er Ten Hong 22crb (petrol, diesel and electricity icons); Stiv Kahlina 55cb; Kathy Konkle 107cra (camera); Mosquito 103bl; Shane O'Brien 106fclb (radio); Tomasz Pietryszek 37tr; T. Popova 104br, 105clb; Vladimir Popovic 58ftl; Laurent Renault 36bl; Petr Stepanov 117cla; Mark Swallow 7bl; Jeremy Voisey 73cra (chemical hazard warning triangle); **Peter Zelei 9tr; Kingspan Off-Site** : 72r; **Massachusetts Institute of Technology (MIT):** Franco Vairani / MIT Smart Cities group 118br, 118cr; **Courtesy of Motorcycle-USA.com:** 37br; **NASA:** 43cr, 54br, 54l, 55tl, 60bl, 119br, 119tr; Finley Holiday Films 48br; SOHO / EIT Consortium / ESA 121tl; **Photolibrary:** 40clb; Hufton + Crow 72bl; Javier Larrea 41tl; Bruno Morandi / Robert Harding Travel 41cr (Trans-Siberian Express); Doug Plummer 102cl; **Press Association Images:** Peter Morrison 115clb; **Reuters:** Albert Gea 103br; **Science & Society Picture Library:** Science Museum 11tl, 13br (socks); **Science Photo Library:** 24br, 44bl, 83cr (contracted pupil); AJ Photo / Hop Americain 90bl; Andrew Lambert Photography 94crb; Alex Bartel 116-117b (house); BSIP, Chassenet 83crb (dilated pupil); Dr. Jeremy Burgess 78crb; Pascal Goetgheluck 91crb, 105br (eye); Gustoimages 57br, 70-71 (fridge x-ray), 95cra, 103tr (mobile phone x-ray); Roger Harris 99tl; Mehau Kulyk 88tl (wave background), 92-93t (background), 103tc; Lawrence Lawry 79b, 122-123b; Andy Levin 56br; R. Maisonneuve, Publiphoto Diffusion 91tc; Jerry Mason 103cla (disassembled mobile phones); Will & Deni McIntyre 85clb; Medical Rf.com 83ca (eye ball), 120tr; Peter Menzel 38br (insert); New York Public Library / Humanities & Social Sciences Library 106tl (Marconi); David Parker 74tl, 114cl; Pasieka 82l, 95bl; Philippe Psaila 38cr, 78l; Pasquale Sorrentino 9tl; Andrew Syred 80bl; Takeshi Takahara 44tr; David Taylor 75cra (light interference), 79tl; Sheila Terry 24bc; Detlev van Ravenswaay 11tc, 55br; **SuperStock:** Prisma 41cra (TGV); **© 2009 Universal Orlando Resort. All Rights Reserved:** 53br; **University of Washington:** Babak Parviz 117br; **Worldwide Aeros Corp.:** 121b.

All other images © Dorling Kindersley
For further information see: www.dkimages.com

Acknowledgments
Dorling Kindersley would also like to thank: Francis Bate, Greg Foot, Leon Gray, Jennifer Lane, Chris Oxlade, and Jon Woodcock for editorial assistance. And thanks to Robert Spanton and Klaus-Peter Zauner from ECS, University of Southampton, for information on Formica robots.